THE
DARK NIGHT
OF THE SOUL

*At least there is hope for a tree: If it is cut down,
it will sprout again, and its new shoots will not fail.*

— JOB 14:7

ALEX KANYI

Job 14:7 (NIV)

At least there is hope for a tree: If it is cut down, it will sprout again, and its new shoots will not fail.

Contents

Disclaimer

This book is written on the basis of my experiences with God. You may want to be aware that God's dealings with all of us are specific to us. Therefore, this book is an advisory one written from a prophetic angle. The information is not gathered from psychologists, counsellors or scientists. All tools were received from various Christian healing streams. Its credibility comes from God and many leaders, professionals, close family and friends who have witnessed my life.

Acknowledgements

This book has come out of my own life journey and struggles. I have sought The Lord for certain answers tailor made to my problems and after years of searching, God began to bring outstanding revelations that have completely changed my life.

My thanks first and foremost go to the Holy Trinity. God is the writer of this book and I would not have made it without Him. Much of my experience in this journey has been mysterious. So much was not logical and understandable to many people around me. By His grace I just followed God's leading and voice in pioneering and journeying to the 'promised land'. Mine has been like an 'Abrahamic Walk' of leaving behind everything I knew. I am just as surprised as anyone else who has witnessed my journey at how God's plans have been unfolding in the midst of chaos, trials, tribulations, failures, weaknesses and ignorance. Truly, God still writes straight in crooked lines. God is the Hero and His absolute genius is unfathomable. Like Bill Johnson says, "to the extent you trust God with mystery, is to the extent He will grant you revelation"[1]. I love you God. I am content and I know that the greatest thing in life is to be your son.

Then I want to thank my wife Rita, who has walked this journey with me for 16 years. She is the one who has suffered most and paid the greatest price following a 'mad man' who never quit searching for answers. Many of these times were very unstable and lonely for her. Often I did not know where I was headed and

---

1   The Value of Mystery, Bill Johnson, Destiny Image Publishers.

I had no language for what I was seeing and sensing. I would not be here without her. She is the most courageous woman I know who stood by me the only way she knew how, often covering my nakedness. Together with my children Tyra and Alex Jr, my family have been my inspiration as they have patiently loved me throughout my journey.

I also want to thank my Parents; The Hon. Nahashon Kanyi and Mrs Anne Kanyi. Your unconditional love, unflinching support and belief in me has been incredible. You have cheered me along all my life. You made hard decisions in partnership with God that have literally been a lifesaver. If you did not send me to the UK, I would not be alive today. You have supported me in every way and have not spared anything or even your very lives to see me succeed. Your wisdom has helped me get out of terrible situations. I honour, love and respect you both. A special thanks to my mum for digging the ground for me and placing a foundation through her intense prayers. I believe I have escaped a lot of darkness through those intercessions. I remember your countless all night prayer sessions over the years; I am truly grateful for this. This is our story and our victory.

I want to give a special thanks to Pastor Grace Kayima of Journey Church Luton and the interns at Greater Works International: Ayanda Phakati, Angelica Davis and Tracy Kayima, who worked tremendously hard on this book. I appreciate your prophetic input, intercessory prayers and for putting in the longest hours researching and sourcing the many spoken messages, journals and prayer ministry notes and then collating that information into intelligible text. You have shown passion and complete dedication to the work of God and this project.

I am grateful to all my friends who have greatly contributed to the success of this book namely Valerie Robie, Alethea Reid and Dr Livingstone Musoro for your time, effort, love and support. Thank you for proof reading, editing and your many suggestions for improvement.

I would like to acknowledge my coach Steven Kasyanenko and his team Tamara Lowe and Jackie Morey for mentoring me, encouraging and advising me. I am grateful for the opportunities you have given me. You have been patient with me; given me much grace and favour to complete this book. I believe our connection is divine and I thank God for all of you.

Then last but not least I say thank you to all who have played a part in my life, whether you realise it or not; even those who were against me, somehow you contributed to this book. So I appreciate those who walked with me and those who walked away. You have all inspired my work, as well as the Holy Spirit.

Endorsements

I congratulate Pastor Alex Kanyi for GOD's Grace upon his work on The Dark Night of the Soul. This is not just another book on the market for Christian books. It is revelatory work in which Pastor Kanyi, who I call Pastor Alex, has shared his life story in a way that is uncovered and vulnerable, yet at the same time courageous and humble. He has used his life story to discuss and teach on a topic that is often not written much about in the Christian circles. Pastor Alex has done this in an unreserved manner that cannot be done without the inspiration of the Holy Spirit.

—Livingstone Musoro, DSc Global Fire Church Luton
Senior Lecturer at London Metropolitan University

Preface

This book is an expression of my experiences. Prophetic words and Seer Journals are at the start of every chapter as they commemorate the chapter in which they appear. These came from prominent leaders at conferences I held or when I attended other conferences. Then some came from my spiritual children when asking God about me. I am amazed at how much God has to say about me, I remember, those moments would always encourage me.

At the end of every chapter there are boxes that are abstractive and summative texts to compliment the content of the chapter. We were seeking God on the structure of this book and God gave us this idea to add an interesting edge to it. I felt it was unusual but as we asked God what to write, it resulted in adding some flavour to the book chapters.

As I faced conflicts and opposition coming against destiny, I had to learn to fight. The 'dark night of the soul' has come out of a rough place. It has been a journey of difficulties and complications, one that cannot be totally understood by many others. I believe that God is raising a new generation of leaders and I am part of that company. He said to me, these leaders are those who will fully be trained, they will not fall but they will restore His face to the church. However, to be this kind of leader one has to go through some 'stripping'. What I mean is that He will make sure you only love and live for Him, by Him removing all dependencies. He wants to be your first companion and friend because the assignments He is giving out are really huge and He knows you need Him in order to stand. This book will then explain how this process worked out for me and what happened as a result.

I believe this season of my life has stretched and strengthened me beyond belief. The person I am today has far more insight, far more revelation and understanding of the path God has set out for me. I have found that the path God sets for us will have obstacles and limitations but not to hinder us, rather to transform us into overcomers. Saints, this book is for you. As I am overcoming so will you too in Jesus's name.

Romans 5:2 – 5 NIV

Through whom we have gained access by faith into this grace in which we now stand. And we boast in the hope of the glory of God. Not only so, but we also glory in our sufferings, because we know that suffering produces perseverance; perseverance, character; and character, hope. And hope does not put us to shame, because God's love has been poured out into our hearts through the Holy Spirit, who has been given to us.

Introduction

1 Peter 4:12-13
Dear friends, do not be surprised at the painful trial you are suffering, as though something strange were happening to you. But rejoice that you participate in the sufferings of Christ, so that you may be overjoyed when His glory is revealed.

'I saw Jesus touching your face and saying son I know you have had a hard life but I will make you forget your troubles for you will see that my blessings are so much more than you can imagine. It will all be worth it. You will forget your tears, your latter days shall be better than your former days. Your unhappiness did not come from me dear; it came from the things the enemy oppressed you with. I am sorry but I am making it alright for you. I know your pain and I know all that you think about. I know your worries and all your fears; I promise I will compensate you greatly'.

[Seer Journal entry from interns, July 2014]

This book is not about doctrine, principles or theology, it is a book about my experience. It details the struggles I have gone through. The pain and the lessons are real, and it is very personal, vulnerable and open. It is my life; it is about my time in the season called the 'dark night of the soul'. God began to take me on a journey and it is that journey that has brought me to this place, where I am able to write this book.

Do you find that no matter what you do, you are unable to move forward in life? Does it seem like nothing you try is working? Do you feel 'stuck' with no hope or feel helpless? You may feel confused without direction and vision. Maybe you have really blown it and you are not sure whether God loves you and you doubt His Love. You are reading this book and you have real fear that you will not fulfil your destiny. My friend you may be experiencing the 'dark night of the soul'. I provide a fuller description of what the 'dark night of the soul' is in Chapter 1 of this book.

I want to talk about what I learned from various Wilderness seasons in my life. The most significant has been this last one that I want to predominantly expound on. I can honestly say that my entire 36 years of existence has felt like a long extended Wilderness experience, interspersed with various deeper 'dark nights of the soul'. I have never felt truly happy. The most painful of all emotions is being unaware of what is wrong or rather feeling that something must be wrong with me and always carrying a sense of not belonging. All my life I carried this and I would not find any answers even as a Christian minister. After many years of leading God's people and helping them I came to a point where I was reaching my end, hitting rock bottom; worn out and tired. It is not the first time that I had been in this place, but this was different. I found myself at a place where I literally had to be forced to receive and I had to depend on others because I was not in a place of giving any more which previously I had been used to for over a decade.

My heart became increasingly filled with fear and filled with this deep sense of rejection. I had come to a place where I had even rejected myself, a place of despair, where I feared this was the end of the road for me and I would lose everything I had given my life to. I became afraid of people and I no longer knew who I could trust. I was haunted by suicidal thoughts and fears of giving up on life. I became someone who was scorned and victimised, I became a pastor who no longer saw that calling, that vision or even saw any hope of it being revived. This was me really settling into the 'dark night of the soul'.

One of the aims of this book is to rekindle hope. I know there are thousands of people just like me, who are exactly where I have been. I know the pain; I know that sense of being lost, I know what it feels like to think God is not with you, to think that God has taken away your calling and your purpose. I know the fears and how real they are. I know what it is to feel stuck and to be unsure of what direction to take. Some of you may be questioning your very foundations of faith; what you have learned up to this point. You are questioning your core values and everything you have held onto for your dear life as it is being shaken.

I know the pain of those who have lost everything, experiencing severe relationship problems and difficulties with loved ones. The very things you have fought for, for many years, you start to watch those things being stripped away; people you have laid your life down for, you start to see those people walk away from you. I have been in situations where my friends walked away and abandoned me. I know what it feels like to be betrayed. I found myself alone, stricken in a bed, feeling weary, tired and unable to escape this sense of weariness; I was burnt out and I no longer had energy.

I had fears of whether God will come through, whether He would still remember me. I had a secret inner desire to just not exist anymore. I had made mistakes and I know what it is like for forces of darkness to come against you. I know what it is like for everything to be exaggerated, to be accused by people and to have the enemy take full advantage of such opportunities to discredit all that you have laboured for in Christ. I know what it is like to lose your reputation and to have to lay your "Isaac" on the altar. I have experienced the death of a vision, not once but twice. Perhaps some of you have experienced the death of a vision even more than I have. So I want to sell hope to you. I want to share my story as openly and as vulnerably as I can. I am including here a prophetic word that the Lord ministered to me at the height of my season of the 'dark night of the soul'.

'The Spirit of the Lord would have me say to you, have I not called you to be a mighty man of war? One whom the Lord says I do not want you to, in this season like Saul did where the great tragedy happened of how the mighty have fallen and he fell upon his own sword. The Spirit of the Lord says son, this is not the time for that, it is not the time for self-accusation, self-putting down, self-analysis and review rather it is the time and the season to even begin to come into areas of trust with Me, says the Lord…I have greater things for you and even though it seems as though you went through this Job season of a stripping, I am getting ready to bring you to a greater equipping but it is almost like the trees that are stripped in the autumn and they almost feel like 'God when is this going to come' and the Lord says son I want to end the frustration that time has brought, by bringing you into My presence that you might be like David who said; and I went into the presence of the Lord, and I beheld their end and saw truly indeed the wealth of the wicked is laid up for the just.'

[Prophetic word, November 2013]

I would like to help you recognise the season you are in and to help you find a way out. I would like to raise awareness of the importance of the season you are in. I want to provide some keys to help you navigate whilst you are in this time of your life. It is crucial that you know that God is still with you in your 'dark night of the soul'.

Contrary to some works that have been published on this topic, I want to tell you today without a shadow of a doubt, that God speaks to those in the Wilderness /'dark night of the soul' and He is actually very talkative! God has been faithful to me, even in times past when I had felt He was not talking to me.

He has come through for me this season and answered many questions that I had from my childhood. God has also surrounded me with a small faithful community. They have suffered alongside me. It has been very difficult for my wife and two children, my parents back in Africa, siblings and spiritual children who chose to cover my nakedness. Though there were times I was more isolated than others, a handful have stood with me through thick and thin. They became the Good Samaritans. They took time to stop and they had enough oil to minister to my wounds as they came along side me. Through journalling and prophetic encouragement, there is not a day that God has not spoken to me throughout this experience. So dear friend there is hope for you. There is a way out. God wants to revive you even while you are still in your 'dark night of the soul'. These are some of the things that I will be sharing in this book.

As the dusk of the day drew closer, he was still alone without the companion he had longed for, that he will share his daily experiences with. All that he had known left him, as if the stench coming from his emotions were too much to still be loved.

Chapter 1

The dark night of the soul

James 1:2-4

Consider it pure joy, my brothers and sisters, whenever you face trials of many kinds, because you know that the testing of your faith produces perseverance. Let perseverance finish its work so that you may be mature and complete, not lacking anything.

'Whatever happens you have chosen in your heart to say I will praise Him and I will not accuse Him for just like Job when he went through difficulties he did not accuse the Lord with his two lips but he stood and he said I will honour Him and I will respect what He chooses to do'.

[Prophetic word, May 2011]

S omeone would ask if the Wilderness is the same as the 'dark night of the soul?' Well, we can say the Wilderness is the season that facilitates the 'dark night of the soul'. It is in the Wilderness that God seizes the opportunity to deal with your soul.

So the 'dark night of the soul' can also be referred to as the 'Wilderness'. My definitions come from the scriptures as well as direct revelation from God. Moreover, I will expound on how and why I entered into the season in the first place.

The 'dark night of the soul' is when one's soul experiences the light of God, which exposes all the hidden things in one's heart. But before that light comes in, one would have already entered into a dark place and season in their life. So then in your soul, it feels like everything hidden is coming up to the surface, these may include life failures, pain, anxieties, anger, loss of ambitions and lost dreams, which can all arise in such a season. The 'dark night of the soul' is a place of unfulfilment, possible compromise in situations, dissatis- faction, failure, fear, loneliness, and a deep longing in your soul. It is when all your dreams seem to have failed, the things you hoped for have all gone, and you are left with nothing in life. It could be imagined as a season of death. Many people think that in this season

God does not speak, they think that God has stopped talking, and you are there alone, and just have to figure out everything on your own. But from my experience, I have noticed that God does talk in this season of the 'dark night of the soul'.

You can perceive this Wilderness period as a place of punishment, where you feel like you are serving a sentence for something wrong you did. But, it is not like that, actually it is a place of healing, promotion and great adjustments for the preparation of your destiny. This season is where God is showing you His love, whereby He is allowing you to walk into His purposes for your life. The Wilderness takes you to a place where you can be trained and equipped for something higher, it is the road to your destiny.

Perhaps you are going through this very thing. You have started out in faith, you felt confident with what the Lord has led you to do, but as you have gone along the journey, you felt like there is no hope, and you feel like giving up. Sometimes it could be losing people that are precious to you, it could be suffering what we call 'labour loss': losing things that you have laid your life down for, and this often happens in the Wilderness. There seems to be a loss, that has to take place in order to gain.

The more you step into destiny, the more there will be Wilderness seasons but they are not there to limit you. They are there to build you up so that you can overcome and progress to a new level. Nevertheless saints, it is easy to get stuck in the Wilderness. If you are not aware of how to pass through, it can seem like it is just repeating itself. As we go on we will look at how to navigate through the Wilderness and the 'dark night of the soul'.

I want to show you that my life was far from pleasant for such a long time. However, I have seen it unfolding in the last couple of years as God began to mend it. Brothers and sisters, the Wilderness is a place of mending and I can testify that this season has been my time of mending, rebuilding and restoration as you will see.

As he sets out to make his way home, his eyes are fixed on his father. His eyes were fixed on reaching the prize of walking in fullness. However, as he walked his days become darker and he found himself in the forest, a great big place where he could only depend on God and where God had to become his number one. As he walked, he realised that his secrets were no longer important, his heart was desperate to become intimate with his father.

Chapter 2

My life story

Jeremiah 29:11
"For I know the plans I have for you," declares the LORD, "plans to prosper you and not to harm you, plans to give you hope and a future

'I see a picture of Alex walking down a path holding sacks of baggage. I see the baggage has a smell and leaves a trail of garbage behind him. I see as he walks and gets tired, God comes to take the bags and he is able to walk freely'

[Seer Journal entry, July 2014]

The biblical account of the life of Jacob is found in the book of Genesis chapters 25-50. Jacob deceives his father Isaac and robs his brother Esau of his inheritance. He, however, still received God's hand of favour and acceptance upon him and God worked with him just as he was.

I believe God always declares the end from the beginning (Isaiah 46:10). He knows all about you and He knows your character, He knows your issues but He completely accepts you, completely embraces you because He believes in His ability to transform you along the way. I believe this is the way God works in all of us and for contextual purposes, I want to share my story with you. This will help you understand how it led me to write this book.

I was born on 14th January 1978. It was a difficult pregnancy for my Mum, I almost died three times, twice before I was born and then once during child birth. Then I had a very sickly and traumatic childhood. I remember not feeling loved, feeling distressed and never being happy. I used to be scorned at and laughed at for bed wetting until I was about 12 years old. I remember being bullied and beaten up by the local boys for being different. My head was too big; my ears were big enough to pick me up like a rabbit. I had a deadly village accent (this was something to be picked on by city boys) and my voice was as shrill as a bird for a boy. I was very shy and that did not do me any favours. But then I learned to fight back and I became quite the bully; bullying my brothers and picking on the weaker people as a child. We lived a very nomad lifestyle as we moved homes so much. I never learned to put down my roots anywhere and neither did I have permanent friends. Throughout my life, I have not been happy. There have always been struggles in my life. I can say my life has been a traumatic one. I experienced the most unusual things in my life since childhood. I grew up with a sense of not belonging; I am an illegitimate child, born of an additional second wife, and this has contributed to feelings of rejection. I believe this same state is what led to my rebellion in my teen years. I used to rebel against my parents, leaders, authority, even rebel against my friends.

I did not grow up as deeply religious. Church life was seasonal or was inconsistent in my early childhood. I was curious about God but I had a sense that I would be a leader but it was misguided. In 1995, aged 17, I decided to seriously give my life to God. In my early twenties I was ordained as a minister in the church. I got married a few years after this. I knew at that time that I was not ready for such church service. I served with many limitations. I had many problems, financial limitations, emotionally unstable, marital problems, sexual problems, etc. It was difficult to lead God's people with these life struggles. Not long after that, I was assigned my first pastorate in Watford, UK. This came with its own issues and all I could think about was whether I qualified to be a pastor. I struggled with many issues in my life whilst always maintaining a deep sense of inadequacy and insufficiency. I want to show you that my life was far from pleasant for such a long time. I gave my life to God on the 3rd of December, in 1995, during a deliverance service. Earlier that year, I had dropped out of school, I had mental challenges and some issues to do with attempting to get involved in a cult in high school. But God was in it all and He did not really allow me to get myself too deep into that. I left school severely depressed, which led me to being institu- tionalised. I was the black sheep of the family. I was suffering a lot. I was suicidal with no purpose and my life was not going anywhere. So when I finally gave my life to God, that same night I experienced my first deliverance service. This was the beginning of my quest for freedom and it was so good to know that deliverance is for today and it is also for believers. This was also the first time I got a prophetic word. The prophecy said that I would be a recording artist and that I would lead the next generation to freedom from the very experiences I had encountered. I have subsequently seen this begin to manifest. My experiences would help lead many people into their destinies. Soon after my salvation experience, doors opened for me and I came to the United Kingdom.

In my early years in the UK I was in and out of church. I found myself with worldly friends and my prodigal-sort-of-life of existence began during the year of 1997. It was an inconsistent way of living. Church experience was dry and there never seemed to be any room for people like me. I felt no one really cared or took time to hear the cries of my heart. This went on until August 2002 when I came back to full faith. I had come to believe that I had committed the unpardonable sin. You see many times I had felt God was withholding from me. In anger I would curse God and blaspheme against Him. I committed myself to Christ so many times that I felt I was playing games with Him. I was not able to keep any commitment I made. There was also no healing and discipleship going on in the churches I found myself visiting. I was sick and tired of it all by this time and was tired of life and running around. So many nights I wept and it was impossible to fully enjoy sin. Each time I got drunk, I would end up preaching to my friends and whosoever cared to listen.

So I came back with a vengeance and zeal; realising how long Satan had deceived me and kept me away from the only one who really understood me and could help me – the Lord Jesus Christ. So I fervently and passionately pursued God, greater understanding and healing; leading to my ordination as a pastor under More Than Conquerors Ministries on the 26th December 2003. Here I became heavily involved in deliverance and physical healing. I then left that Ministry after a couple of years and I was leading my own church independently for a while called Kingdom Fellowship. Then in 2006 I submitted my ministry under the Redeemed Christian Church of God (RCCG). The RCCG is a Pentecostal holiness Word of Faith movement. This was one of the most significant seasons of my life, firstly because God supernaturally lead me to RCCG through a series of 15 very clear and specific dreams. By the time I left RCCG in 2009 all these 15 dreams had come to pass. Including the fact that I would only be there for a season. I was ordained, given good spiritual grounding, and an expansive overview of my destiny and vision through in-depth mentoring.

Alongside the ministerial development I have mentioned above God was leading me into a better understanding of inner healing. I had come to see that deliverance on it's own was not adequate enough to bring total and lasting freedom. For this reason I was also attending other church conferences and training events. Some of these ministries included Ellel Ministries, Partners In Harvest, Christian International Europe, Elijah House and Restoring The Foundation. Through these ministries God was building a better understanding of the Father's heart and love, inner healing and training and equipping. Some of these are a part of the new apostolic reformation. As the years unfolded I became a part of some of these organisations and seasons would end and I would find myself leaving one group for various reasons then joining another group and hanging out there, receiving and just being fed for a season. During those times when I led God's people, it seemed like I was dishing out to the people my experiences, what I was going through at that time. God was dealing with me, but I was not fully aware of it, I just followed the leading of my heart. In all these, healing has been the centre of my search. And those who gathered around me were people who needed the food I was dishing out.

I hit rock bottom in 2009 entering a Wilderness season and I was forced to close down my church in Watford. Nothing could have prepared me for this. I was devastated and I had let many people down. I was burnt out and simply could not continue after 5 years of pastoring that church. At the same time I had also been learning and experiencing different expressions of 'church' through the ministries mentioned above. These new revelations made it difficult to remain within a denominational setting. It was a time of transition. Prior to closing the church in 2009, the Lord had led me to start an interde- nominational ministry called Greater Works International (GWI) in 2008. This ministry has been a true reflection of the transition I was going through.

At the height of this Wilderness season (May 2009 - May 2011), I met a much-respected prophetic woman of God on 7th April 2010. I attended her meeting thinking that she would tell me that I am not called and it is time to quit and wrap it up, but she ended up giving me huge prophetic words and promises from God. The vision of GWI that God was developing was strengthened through these prophetic words. I felt affirmed in my calling and after all I was not crazy. I felt very encouraged, and over a year later, in May 2011, I planted a church called Journey Church as part of the church planting initiative of GWI.

With the new church plant I was really determined and excited about how God had given me a new lease of life. The church was growing well and we had many effective tools to help people. God also kept giving us favour with many leaders and churches and God released so much impartation from various revival leaders. More and more answers to the biggest questions I had about life were beginning to unravel. This was the best place I had been or so I thought at the time. I had been in this place of heaviness and mourning from 1995, many, many years of waiting and longing and seeking answers, seeking solutions, seeking the truth and true lasting freedom. It was really a long road, a dark road for most of that time, many things were not in place but having to serve and lead God's people with many limitations in life; financial, familial and even in ministry. I had been faithful with what God had given me despite all these. I had led with my heart in much vulnerability and openness. Receiving public affirmation of my journey and ministry was absolutely amazing and encouraging. But nothing could have prepared me for the 'dark night of the soul' that was coming. I had learned along the way not to accuse the Lord, I had learned to be silent and just love and serve His people. I knew there was nowhere else to go, but that the Lord would indeed somehow answer.

As the Wilderness season began its onset, I first started to notice that I was not as enthusiastic as I was before with my service to the Lord and to His people. (This process will be explained properly in the next chapter.) Eventually, I felt completely worn out. I tried to rest but I could not snap out of it. Nothing I tried helped me to get out of this place of despair. People around me began to really pray for me. Then the Lord asked me to take a rest from ministry, and asked that I let others rise up and take on most of the work. Then everything began to unfold, in this place of great vulnera- bility, weakness, pain and death. It was in this place that God began to really come through for me in what has been the most difficult season of my entire life.

As the soldier rested his feet on a mountain, many children gather around to hear the story that roars within and many children are intrigued by the experiences shared.

Chapter 3

Experiences of the dark night of the soul

Psalms 91:1-5
Whoever dwells in the shelter of the Most High will rest in the shadow of the Almighty. I will say of the LORD, "He is my refuge and my fortress my God, in whom I trust." Surely He will save you from the fowler's snare and from the deadly pestilence He will cover you with His feathers, and under His wings you will find refuge, His faithfulness will be your shield and rampart. You will not fear the terror of night, nor the arrow that flies by day.

The Spirit of the Lord says even if you have felt like an isolated branch, the Lord says you are not an isolated branch, rather you are a remnant says the Spirit of God a stump that is still in the ground'.

[Prophetic word, May 2014]

I invite you to see and perhaps experience with me some of the things I went through in this time. Let me take you step by step, revealing my emotions and my circumstances as I settled into the Wilderness and sunk deeper into the 'dark night of the soul'. I am hoping that you will recognise your season through my story and be at peace knowing that you are not alone. This season is a place of intense loneliness but this is also the time to know the Holy Spirit. Many do not survive or navigate well through these periods of their lives, the temptations and devastations are too much.

I will be talking about my emotional state at the time. You will see emotions highlighted such as depression, shame, failure, guilt, etc. Emotions were the biggest part of that period because the enemy really maximised them and tormented me intensely, taking me into the darkest parts of the season. In this chapter you will see how everything kept crumbling before me as the Lord stripped away everything I had. He allowed friends to abandon me. He allowed chaos to explode among my loved ones and I saw my Ministry crushing before me. I realised that the essence of the Wilderness is that He removes all dependencies from you, leaving only Him to depend on. This is what the Bible means when it says Jacob was left limping (Genesis 32:22-24)

The Stages of the Dark Night of the Soul

I want to take you back through the various events that contributed and led me into the 'dark night of the soul'. I found myself faced with a variety of tests. By 2013 my calling in life was rather clear and I had tried my best to pursue God and do the calling the best I could. But the Lord usually breaks His servants and takes them through a time of refining before He would use them and hand them their inheritance, for me this was the case. Now I understand that my calling and beliefs had to be tested, and so there was a price to pay. With each test that I encountered the question was, "Am I still going to serve God diligently?"

An example of this was about being a Spiritual Father to many. I really took great honour in this and I loved being a father. So one question I constantly heard from the Lord is "Will you still be a father?"

Loss of a Loved One

My relationship with my mother for the most part was a good one. Nevertheless, when things were bad they were really bad. When we were on good terms, it was good enough for me to allow her to sit in my very first counselling session as I confessed all my sins. My mother has always been there for me in an advisory capacity, has always been supportive no matter how bad the situations became. She has helped me get through the 'dark night of the soul', fought alongside me and has been consistently interceding for me. Unfortunately, I was separated from my family from the age of 17 when I left my motherland of Kenya for the shores of the British Isles. Sometime later in 2010, I met a family that began to take interest in our ministry; 'Mama Miriam,' as we

15

fondly called her and her two daughters. She was unwell and had battled cancer for a while. I spent the next two years supporting her, we became good friends, she looked after me and she always served my favourite strawberry and vanilla ice-cream whenever I visited her. Mama Miriam understood me and could always tell when I was hurting. You see as a pastor I was always the giver and for the first time someone was really paying attention to me. She treated me as a son to a large extent. I enjoyed being with her, taking her shopping and other practical things when she needed help. Unknowingly, I had always longed for a mother figure whilst in the UK; someone who would look after me, nurture me and accept me. I found myself always escaping the pressures of life at her home. It felt amazing to be there and she would make me feel at home, make me breakfast and share stories passionately. Sadly in 2012, Mama Miriam passed away. I felt as though God had pulled away just what my heart was longing for. You see, I had never grieved for anyone in my life. I grew up hating funerals and never cried as we laid to rest many loved ones over the years. I had a very cold and unloving heart of stone. I was numb and did not feel much pain. God had been dealing with my heart over the years but this time something happened.

After the funeral the grief was so intense I almost felt suicidal. It was the first funeral I had conducted as a minister. She had also asked that I look after her daughters after she was gone. I never expected that she would die even at the last minute. We had felt as if God had assured us of her recovery. This is where I believe my season of the 'dark night of the soul' started. I just felt my life spiral downwards; I felt all the energy and strength inside my heart leave. All I wanted was someone who would protect me, look after me and allow me to be myself. I was usually the one who protected and rescued those around me taking responsibility for their lives and actions. Mama Miriam was also becoming a mother figure in the church. I longed for mothers in our church, strong ladies who would teach the girls how to be women. What I learned is that through her death God was asking me, "will you be a father without the help of mothers?"

Depression

After the death of Mama Miriam, it felt as though a can of worms had been unleashed. I could feel pain that I had not experienced before; deep pain with feelings of abandonment and rejection. My heart was bleeding, I felt so alone and unprotected as though I had to defend and protect myself. I could see myself falling down a slippery slope of depression; the pain in my heart was so deep and so raw. Being alone in this country for years without my mum stirred up a deep longing in my heart for a mother figure. I also felt childhood pain; where my mum was emotionally absent, Mama Miriam in some ways filled that void, but now she was gone and the scars from my childhood had been unleashed.

Moral Failure

This was the next major event that happened and is one of the most difficult times I endured. I never thought I would ever find myself in the predicament I was in. I fell immorally with someone who was very close to me. It became a time of great distress and I felt as though I was robbed of a testimony. I had prided myself in having no secrets and here I was now consumed with a lot of guilt, and the heaviness of having to keep a secret. I felt as though I had failed myself, the world, my family, the community and those who trusted me. I felt like I was the scum of the earth, like God had given me this amazing call but now I had ruined it. I felt like Adam, rejected from the Garden of Eden due to sin and hiding. Even though I had confessed my sin to a fellow minister and he told me that God had forgiven me, I was still living in guilt as I had to wear 'fig leaves' amongst my inner circle. The question that consumed me was, "am I still called to be a father?"

Resting

Not long after the moral failure, I found myself becoming weary and tired. I am not usually one who gives into the needs of my flesh; I would serve my spiritual children for over 12 hours a day and still had the energy to keep going until the early hours of the morning. However, this weariness was unusual, no matter how much I slept it just never seemed to be enough. I asked my spiritual children to ask God for me what was happening to me, He simply replied, "Dear you are becoming tired because I am asking you to rest and spend time with Me, allow Me to look after your church". At this point the tiredness was so intense. Subsequently, I found it difficult to rest; I was used to being a busy person making this unusual for me. I handed the church to the care of my spiritual daughter who has served me faithfully now for 10 years. However, whilst I was in my Wilderness my failure became public.

Rejection by Spiritual Children

I took pride in having spiritual children; to me they were my family and my heroes. I had invested my life in seeing that they would become all that they were created to be. I will never forget the day that I took my children to Leeds, UK, and they were given a chance to prophesy over the congregation of my best friend's church of about 500 members. It was beautiful to see them move in the things of the Spirit. Little did I know that it would be the last time I would ever see many of them again, the last time we were a family. As soon as we got back from that trip my sin was exposed and there was uproar. My sin deeply wounded all those who had grown to love me, all those whom I had served diligently and passionately. I loved them with my whole heart and now I was the one who had deeply wounded them. They were scared and it was as if their worlds had crashed before their eyes. My guilt and shame began to eat me up more than anything; I was the one who was responsible for this pain. I wanted to hold them and reassure them that everything would be ok; I wanted to show them how sorry I was, to show them my heart and show them that I never meant to break theirs. But I could see the anger and rage in their hearts projected through their eyes, I could see disappointment glare at me. I had lost all I had built; I had lost those I wanted nothing but the best for. My heart had always been to raise them up and release them into destiny and now I had to let go of them prematurely. I was left with the question, "do I still want to be a father?", even if my children had rejected me.

Ministerial Rejection

After the exposure of my failure, I felt a relief; I was able to seek help from the inner healing leaders around me. I knew that I had a problem that only God could save me from. I went around to all my pastor friends and explained to them what had happened. I needed counsel, guidance and support. I was greatly disappointed when I experienced a lack of support from ministerial leaders. Many leaders rejected me, others tried to help but from a distance, no one actually became a good Samaritan to help build me up again. My ministry, my family and my life were on the line, not one of my pastoral leaders could walk alongside me and be a friend. It was a painful process but God wanted to know whether I could be a father even when my fellow pastors had rejected me. He was asking me whether I was willing to stand out. God actually said that "the more you say yes to Me, the more you will be rejected".

Isolation

I have never been one who likes to spend a lot of time alone, I love the company of other people, the security and the communion that is shared in the presence of others. As I had reached this place of isolation it was as if God had abandoned me and left me to die. I was already feeling as though the world around me had crumbled. I had lost everything that I had built my life upon and now I found myself stuck in a big house to be reminded of my failures. When I asked God why have you abandoned me? He simply said "son, I am using your natural children to show you my unconditional love, to them you are still perfect and you are still a father." Suddenly my eyes were opened to see that God was rebuilding my confidence as a father. He was drawing my biological children closer to me to show me that even though I was not perfect in the eyes of man, I was perfect in the eyes of God and that was all that mattered.

Family Separation

I had never seen anyone so beautiful and perfect until the day I held my daughter, I had feelings in my heart that were new, I had never known a love like this. I remember whispering to God, 'what is this?' and I sensed Him saying 'this is unconditional love'. As I held my new born baby, it felt as though my life was complete. I can honestly say my daughter taught me how to love, how to be a better man. The only other time in my entire life when I had experienced unconditional love was when I was 13 years old and was hospitalised as I suffered from tonsillitis. When my family came to visit me, I experienced a wave of love as it was the first time I had felt that overwhelming sense of value. As I mentioned earlier, all my life my heart was incapable of loving, it was numb and cold. I did not know what unconditional love was. My parents loved their children and there was nothing to suggest that I was not loved. I believe we can all know that we are loved but not have the experience of that love deep in our hearts. I was a very dysfunctional individual and I deeply struggled to have love and affection for my loved ones. I often wondered what was wrong with me and why I was different. To me my daughter was the best thing that happened to me. She gave me a reason to live and I burned with new feelings of love and admiration I had never experienced before. Years later my son was born and those feelings of unconditional love expanded out to him. I really love my kids; they are a huge part of my world.

So when circumstances led to me no longer being able to see my children, my whole world fell apart. It felt like I had a hole in my heart. I could feel myself slowly dying, the pain was unbearable. I would do anything for my children. I will never hurt or reject them, my children were my world and my everything. I was over protective of them; I never imagined a day would come when I would not watch them sleep each night. I never thought I could live without them. To make matters worse, many people accused me of running away from my problems and of abandoning my children. Very few things in life have hurt me to this extent.

The pain was so much I would just sleep with deep heaviness over my head. For several months I shut down. By this time I was in need of personal resurrection. I would constantly ask God, "God why my children? Why are you breaking me completely?" And He would respond "what about now? When you don't have your biological children? Will you still be a father? Will you still raise my children?" God began to speak to me about how my children had taken first place in my heart and that I needed to be completely stripped so I would come to the place of realising that He is the only one I needed in life. I saw that I had no one but God and He was my true and only companion. He wanted me to find contentment in being His son. This needed to be enough and this was and is my true identity. God was leading me to a place of absolute trust in Him and Spiritual intimacy.

Rebuilding

God brought me to a place in my life where I had my face flat on the floor and I had both hands up in surrender. I said God have your way with me. I had nothing left, I had no income, no savings, no friends, no family, I was a broken man, with nothing to really live for. My heart and prayer began to change and I would weep so much and beg Him to let me live for His Glory and the honour of His name. All I desired now was to be His son. I was finally beginning to fully yield to anything and everything that He had for me. Without God, it was impossible to get out of the total mess I was in.

Persecution and Accusations

In the midst of the full effects of the 'dark night of the soul' I experienced a huge amount of persecution and accusations. Persecution came when my moral failure was exposed. The story slowly spread in my Ministry within a small group before it was presented to me. Once I was confronted, the story spread across many communities and even reached my home town, Nairobi, Kenya through the publication of a newspaper article. During these times I was experiencing great depression and an overwhelming darkness. The more I learned of the rumours, the more I became depressed. I was traumatised. I had hurt my family, spiritual children and I was being publically disgraced by those who were once my friends and even those who did not particularly know me. I felt like I had nowhere to turn. I felt alienated, betrayed, like an abandoned soldier left in the battlefield to die. I began to feel the weight of everything I had carried through ministry come down on me. I was feeling suffocated by my current state but everything began to intertwine and I was left feeling a substantial level of heaviness. I was in a place where I had never been and I doubted if I would ever recover. I could not see a way out and I felt like I was losing myself as well as everyone and everything around me.

I lay in bed most days and nights suffering from insomnia. I could no longer hide behind church activities and people. This forced me to face myself and reflect upon my life thus far. I knew that God had taken me out of the dirt and He had truly saved me but then the question of my heart was why did God bring me here? Although I had taken responsibility for my mistakes and accepted the consequences, I had questions for the Lord in that I had cried to Him for years to deliver me from these same weaknesses. This was the hardest part for me. I had walked vulnerably before the church about my issues and many people were being set free as a result of feeling loved, accepted and understood in their own weaknesses. Yet my deliverance was not quite complete and I had faithfully done my best to serve the Lord while being a 'leper'.

I could identify with the story of Naaman in 2 Kings 5. He was the commander of the armies of Syria while having leprosy. This was a humbling experience for him, all along the answer was in his house right 'under his nose'. His maid would later tell of a prophet in Israel who had power to heal him. Arriving at the door step of Prophet Elisha, further 'humiliating acts' for this great general finally saw his skin restored to that of a young child. This was my story, only for me I ended up blowing it before my encounter with the great physician—Jesus. Why did God allow me to sink this far?

After some time, I started getting threats from local witchcraft covens trying to inflict me with sickness and death. This happened on several occasions. Some people who had heard of my name informed some friends of mine. For me this was all too much, things could not have gotten any worse. I had a rush of thoughts come to me, 'why do they want me?' 'What have I done to them?' 'How did they find me?' I asked a few church leaders to pray for me but they did not believe this was actually happening. This made me feel even more isolated. However, a few months later God confirmed through a proven prophet that an opposition came against me in the work of the occult. This really opened my eyes to see that the enemy was really after my life. But it also made me stronger, it made me realise that the attacks were bigger than I first thought and I was able to come to terms with the fact that I was in a spiritual battle.

I became afraid for my family and my own life during that time. Nevertheless, it was an opportunity for me to see how God was protecting me. Therefore, in the midst of all the fear I also had an inner peace and I just knew that God was fighting for me. Although I had been rejected by people, God was always hinting to me that He was still fighting for me and He was still on my side. He had a bigger plan that I had not fully comprehended yet. I was able to see my worth and that the enemy sought to destroy me. Therefore, although I felt like I deserved to be rejected, there was more to it. God was showing me that I was called for such a time as this.

A few months later I regained a little strength to pick myself up and do what God had put on my heart but an alarming dream came to me. I learned that another storm was coming my way. This storm would be based on the opinion of others and their perceptions. The Lord revealed that it would be called accusations. The purpose of this was also to discredit my calling as a father. When the storm hit it rocked my world. It was extremely painful and there were times I would wonder if I was doing the right thing. I knew what God was putting on my heart was from Him but the accusations really caused me to lose faith. I was receiving mixed counsel and advice. However, prophecies were encouraging me to continue, yet the advice of others caused me to believe I was delusional. I can say God truly led me through all this. If it was not for His surprises and His demonstration of unconditional love I would not have been able to persevere. Yet out of all this the love of God has empowered me to be a better father to my spiritual children, I have learned a lot more about myself, my children and my wife through them.

All the things that God was putting on my heart were big and although I did not particularly understand everything, an inner strength formed within me. I learned to completely rely on God. Through His voice, God guided me through this time, and not only did God tell me what was on the way, He also directed and guided me at every step and every stage. Day to day I was hearing what He was saying to me. I know that I would not have been able to get through without Him. God was teaching me that He is my support system. Where people turned away, God never turned away, and He did not leave me to suffer on my own.

Here is an encouraging prophesy from the Lord I received in the midst of my pain.

"Son, I love you.

He puts out His hands and He says, all your worries and burdens are in My hands.

I promise you that you will never be alone. You will always have a companion. I am your companion. I have taken you through all of this, just to come and show you that I wanted to be your companion. I had to take everything away, so that there are no distractions, so that I am the only one you can depend on. So that I am the only one you can look to.

You cannot look to your children, your wife, your ministry or your spiritual children. Everything I have mentioned has disappointed you and I did it on purpose. And as you begin to realise that I am your friend, I want you to get closer to Me, there is a prize at the end.

Son, recognise the season, it is not the season to look at the things that have disappointed you. It is not the season to question your circumstances and say why has this gone wrong. It is a season for you to get it, for you to get that I am the one to look to. When you look to Me you will see that all your questions are answered. I am the one who does not give many details, but My parables are enough to keep you on track.

I saw you small and locked up in a bottle. Father God closed the lid. Father said, this is how you feel, stuck, suffocated and like you cannot get out. In all this I am the Prince of Peace. I had to bring you to this place, if you look at your life before this season, you will see that you did everything else but you did not look to Me.

I honour you for your hard work; I recognise you and I love you for it. But in this season, it is not about what you do, it is about who you are and who I want you to be, it's to be a son. That is why I brought you here.

It is just that Sonship requires everything. Do you not see that Jesus had to lose everything? Even while on earth, he had to lose everything. He had to grow into proper Sonship. He is your example. So do not worry about what you have lost. I am giving you a chance to gain me. I am so much more than those things."

(Seer Journal Entry, 2014)

Finally, God began to show me that what is in my hand is what He would use to rebuild me. What I have is my story and the various tools and answers that I have learned on my Journey. As this season of the 'dark night of the soul' began to set in, God used to tell me that He was the one who would restore me. Restoration for me was about coming to a place of intimacy with the Lord. Intimacy comes out of the position of being a son before our heavenly Father, which is based on trust. Over the years, God had increasingly added tools for inner healing and deliverance. Even though I had many years of experience in this, nothing could have prepared me for the level of bondage and brokenness I encountered in that season. I have had countless prayer ministry sessions and each time God went deeper and deeper revealing mysteries of the Kingdom of Darkness. There are reasons why many believers live out their entire Christian lives with many limitations. These limitations also hinder true intimacy with God and have countless Christians trapped in religion. I will describe my healing process more fully. Intimacy, healing, identity and rest were the instructions He had for me in this season of the 'dark night of the soul'. I was to be in a place of receiving and for a hard working dedicated rescuer; this was a very hard thing to do. But I had no choice and no energy to do anything else. Looking back now, God has given me a life that I was never going to have otherwise.

Jesus said in Luke 14:26, "if any man comes to me and does not hate his own father and mother and wife and children and brothers and sisters, yes even his own life, he cannot be my disciple." I have come to live this scripture. In God's Kingdom, you lose to gain.

As soldier endures, through absolute darkness, he endures the curse man has placed on him, the labels they stick on his forehead as he sets out to do what seems like the impossible to men but the possible through God. As he labours to serve God's people the fire of God arose inside of him. He began to see God in his true armour; his eyes begin to open to the love of God and he learns to trust God wholeheartedly.

Chapter 4

My healing process

Psalm 107:19-21 NIV
Then they cried to the Lord in their trouble, and he saved them
from their distress. He sent out his word and healed them; he
rescued them from the grave. Let them give thanks to the Lord
for his unfailing love and his wonderful deeds for mankind.

'I like that you are running to Me, I am ready to heal you. I have taken everything you were holding onto, everything you were depending on so that you can see Me only and now you are on the right path running to Me. You are where I wanted you to be. I am ready to heal you'

[Seer Journal entry, 2013]

Healing Process

The restoration or healing of the heart is one of our ministry's core values. The heart is the jugular vein of Christianity and the enemy knows very well that he only needs to choke and afflict our hearts through unfortunate life experiences, and Christianity becomes a mere religion like all others. I believe that true Christianity touches and transforms our hearts, and it is the only faith that touches the hearts of men. The Bible says a lot about the heart.

'The heart is deceitful above all things and beyond cure. Who can understand it?' (Jeremiah 17:9).

This scripture shows that we never know the full depths of our issues, only God can reveal them to us. God intends to heal our hearts so that we can walk in communion with him at an intimate level.

'I will give them a heart to know me that I am the Lord. They will be my people, and I will be their God, for they will return to me with all their heart.' (Jeremiah 24:7)

Over time, I had discovered that I could not fully give my heart to God. My heart was too cold, incapable of giving or receiving love. My life experiences had taught me to close my Heart to people and to God. It meant that my spiritual life could not progress to a place of success. I had searched for answers for such a long time and yet nothing brought permanent healing. During that time, God was using me to bring healing to others, the same healing that I desperately needed. I had not known His plan all along. Father God was showing me things about myself, my past and family through my spiritual children.

God said, 'What you see in them is what is in you and your family and I will heal you as you heal them'.

That promise left me in a bit of an epiphany realizing that I had to be patient with God in order to be healed. So when my season of healing had finally dawned on me, I felt overwhelmingly ecstatic and relieved. I could say that healing was a fundamental stage of the season of the 'dark night of the soul'. It was a turning point that brought great insight and lasting revelation to me and my ministry. I will never forget, at the worst point in my entire life, with all the shame and fear, failure and ridicule I was going through, God said,

'Son the time has come, I am coming to heal you and I will completely restore you even in this season'.

Finally I began to receive answers I had waited for all my life. God showed me His unconditional love even as my whole world crumbled. He did not judge me or condemn me. It was hard to accept His love at first but I had nowhere to go and no one else to look to. He became my one and only source of help. There were various healing avenues I had come across and out of them God healed me in a way that produced some rather astonishing results as you will see. That is how I knew that God had given me something different and unique. It was an unconventional form of healing that was not known or popular in my circles.

Alter Personalities

One of the key things that God revealed to me is that I had alter personalities. An Alter is an alternative personality or part of a human personality. They are also called hurt parts and their purpose is to aid and empower the person to deal with a specialized situation which was difficult, painful or traumatic. However, all alters create rights to the enemy and get attached to the demonic realm. Alters are created unknowingly by the individual, often in childhood.

I can confidently say that my healing would have not been complete without this revelation. It changed my whole life. God amazed me with how he used it to set me free. Before this as I have re-iterated throughout this book, nothing much worked out for me in over 17 years of searching! I found out that I had hundreds of alter person- alities and from then on the healing has been dramatic. Some alters include fear, self-protection, shame, control, perversion, hatred of men, hatred of women, suicide and many others. This also unlocked the demonic that attaches to these alters and week after week I was experiencing glorious freedom and transformation. However, this new understanding of alter personalities revealed a far more sinister force of darkness and I want to unpack this unknown enemy next.

Unknown Enemy

I had come to a place where I had to discover what this unknown enemy was, after living a life that did not make sense and experiencing things that could not be explained or were not logical. I kept seeking after God's heart to find out what this could be; it seemed to be beyond all natural limitations, beyond what my mind could imagine. After some time, God started showing me what was behind my altar personalities. It's something I had heard of but I had not come to know it to this extent. This unknown enemy is what we call the spirit of Jezebel.

The back drop of this revelation

It all began in 2004 at a Prophetic Seers Conference in Dudley, England, where I was given a prophetic word about the 5 stones of David (1 Samuel 17:40). These 5 stones would represent five demonic strongholds that have crippled lives and nations and how God would use me to raise leaders who would in turn help me bring down these strongholds. This prophecy gripped my heart and the Lord constantly kept on reminding me of it. I diligently sought the Lord over the years about its true meaning and I have patiently watched as this prophetic word has unfolded piece by piece over the last decade. The 5 stones are as follows: 1. Jezebel/Ahab; 2. Witchcraft; 3. Sexual perversion, 4. Mammon/ poverty and 5. Fear.

These are the main areas that have worked against me in my life. God has revealed how these strongholds use inherited generational spirits (disembodied spirits) in all of us and alter personalities to program us below the radar and keep us in bondage and cycles. This is what has unlocked my life and the lives of other unlikely champions. This revelation is the main reason the enemy attempted to wipe me out! So that He was not exposed.

The Five Stones

1(a) The Spirit of Jezebel

Note for qualifying Jezebel: Jezebel is an evil spirit and therefore is neither male nor female, but for ease of reference, throughout this book I refer to it as 'her' or 'she' due to the origination of the name being closely tied with the biblical character who was King Ahab's wife. I will also give biblical examples of men in the Bible that had the spirit of Jezebel.

There are two passages where the name 'Jezebel' appears; first in 1 Kings 18:4 as a vicious monarch who attacked and killed prophets of God, then in the last book of the New Testament Revelation 2:20. These were two women who lived centuries apart so there is no way they could be the same person. We can safely say they are two different people who were possessed by the same spirit. Today we call this, the spirit of Jezebel.

The spirit of Jezebel is a demonic principality that comes into an individual's life through witchcraft and the occult, sexual perversion, false religions, and fatherlessness, this can also be inherited genera- tionally. The person involved will begin to show traits of Jezebel which are mainly pride, insecurity, jealousy, lust, malice, hatred, abuse, self-protection and fear. These traits can be seen in men as well as women. It is important to understand that the spirit of Jezebel cannot operate without an Ahab spirit. All human beings have been affected by the Jezebel and the Ahab spirit. All of us have controlled others and have been controlled by others. Another way of looking at it is that we all can have passive, passive aggressive or aggressive tendencies.

One of the main keys that began to break/dismantle this was the prophetic seer realm. We had begun training people in the area of hearing the voice of God and prophetic activations. It so happened that many in our team were very prophetically gifted and were actually seers (See 1 Samuel 9:9; 2 Kings 17:13; 1 Chronicles 21:9). We see Jesus flowing in this seer prophet dynamic in John 5:19 and it is a pattern for all believers. God gave us a revelation that Lucifer uses Jezebel and Mammon as his biggest perpetrators against mankind. He uses them to control the world and the nations. Mammon is a spirit that rules and reigns over money. It is a spirit that mirrors greed, tends to run the financial systems of the world and destroys businesses because people fail to trade with integrity. Unfortunately, Christians have fallen into this trap and this affects church finances. This spirit makes people focus on money rather than God. That's one way to recognize that you are completely tied to the spirit.

'No one can serve two masters. Either you will hate the one and love the other, or you will be devoted to the one and despise the other. You cannot serve both God and money' (Matthew 6:24).

On the other hand, Jezebel aims to be the counterfeit of the Holy Spirit; I have witnessed this in many healing sessions. The purpose is so that you are unable to connect with the true God and instead succumb to the false intimacy she brings.

We can see the Jezebellic nature in the Garden of Eden where Satan stopped the flow of true intimacy and replaced it with rationalism. This is her strongest hold on mankind. Rationalism is defined as "Reliance on reason as the basis for establishment of religious truth; a theory that reason in itself is a source of knowledge superior to and independent of sense perceptions." (Webster's New Collegiate Dictionary).

When we rationalize God's word it kills intimacy with Him and brings fear rather than faith. Intimacy is trust. Adam and Eve were enticed to rationalize God's instructions whereas prior to that they had enjoyed continuous spiritual connection with God and totally depended on Him. From this point, man could no longer trust God and religion was birthed.

The Lord showed me that rationalism has become a 'god' especially in the western nations. In one of my healing sessions, we discovered that rationalism could also be an alter personality. The fact that we can have a hidden alter called rationalism goes to show the extent to which the enemy will use it just to hinder intimacy with God. For me, the alter personality of rationalism held on to my family traditions and culture, as well as religion and in particular my Catholic background. These ideas and philosophies were so indented into my heart and soul. As a result it limited me from fully embracing God's culture, God's words and receiving the prophetic. We could see Jezebel fleeing from that place. Out of all alters that the Lord has healed me from, rationalism, sexual perversion and identity had been the biggest Jezebel strongholds.

1(b) Ahab

We cannot talk about Jezebel without mentioning Ahab. The two work in conjunction with one another. As we know, Ahab was Jezebel's husband. As Jonas Clarke pointed out:

'Ahab is best known for his provoking spirit. Scripture says, "Ahab did more to provoke the Lord God of Israel to anger than all the kings of Israel that were before him" (1 Kings 16:33). Can you imagine inflaming the Lord to such a degree that He would pen such a legacy for you?

That makes it crystal clear how the Lord feels about the Ahab spirit. To provoke means to anger, irritate and annoy'.

People with Ahabic tendencies are open to the spirit of Jezebel which gives them false comfort and assurance. Ahabic people may appear to be strong and can be conquerors, Presidents and Kings but in actual fact they are weak, completely controlled and manipulated by the spirit of Jezebel. These spirits are co-dependent, whereas Jezebel tends to be more vicious and bold, Ahab usually operates as a 'victim'. However, Jezebel can remain dormant for years in an individual until something triggers it off. So these individuals can appear quite passive in some roles and areas of life and then similarly someone who is predominately Ahab can act quite aggressive when threatened, and in those instances they may seem more Jezebelic. Someone with Ahab characteristics, tend to look for and align with big and bold people to make him feel big and strong. This is the sort of person who will drive himself crazy as he has no idea how to stand alone.

Both Jezebel and Ahab spirits come in because of great pain and hurt mainly experienced in our childhood. People with the spirit of Jezebel are usually more wounded than their Ahab counterparts. From my experience, people under the influence of Jezebel find it harder to seek help. They hate change and genuinely don't seem to recognize their wounds, especially early childhood ones. It's also extremely difficult for them to face themselves; they keep an illusion of perfection and hardly apologize or admit their wrongs. It is always someone else's fault. For this reason, it's unfortunate that many never recover from this.

It is commonly agreed that there are way more people in the world that have the spirit of Ahab than those who have the spirit of Jezebel. Other traits of Ahabic people include indecisiveness and a tendency to put responsibility on others. In addition, they tend to have identity issues for they struggle to understand themselves, otherwise they would not tolerate the spirit of Jezebel (Revelations 2:18-29). True freedom for Ahabic people is found when they come to know and accept their identity in Christ. The same applies to Jezebel.

Through the process of healing, God has revealed all these things. As a result, many mysteries and questions about my life have been uncovered and will continue to be uncovered. This is the dynamic that I grew up in; it's all I have ever known in life, in church, in marriage and all my years in ministry. It was all around me. It was inherited as my parents and the generations before them all operated in this Ahab/Jezebel dynamic. Most men in my family were actually more like Ahab while the women were very much like Jezebel. These are the women the men of my family married and found themselves attracted to. Our women attracted Ahabic men without any exception. These things may not be readily visible at first, but as I grew in healing it became easier and easier to see it everywhere. Even in the ministry, many leaders are plagued by this. It's all over in the media as well all driven by misogyny and misandry.

It was crushing to face myself too; this was a major issue in my life! Some of the Ahabic traits that I bore were passivity, indecisiveness, dependency, self-willed, stubborn, reckless, heartless, judgmental and argumentative. I battled clinical depression for many years and it could be triggered by little things. The sadness could be exaggerated by small things and I can get so upset quickly. This is how King Ahab was and that's why they say he was provoking. Another Ahab trait in my life was that I had a tendency of not addressing things immediately. This has affected me so much especially with my long-term relationships in the ministry because it nearly cost me faithful ministers as they found it almost impossible to transition from one level to another. This is also because of another important point to note about Ahabs; 'Ahab's' are blinded and cannot see what Jezebel is really like. This is how King Ahab in the Bible survived Queen Jezebel. He had some inclinations that something was off but he was too passive to really know what she was really like. When the Lord opened my eyes to this, I was so traumatized at the depth of blindness to Jezebel on my part and how much I had allowed people to use and abuse my time and resources. I had no boundaries and surrounded by the Jezebel/ Ahab dynamic, I was often left dry and empty.

Ahab is also full of anger and resentment and a key reason is that they constantly give out and never seem to receive back. It was extremely difficult for me to face this, realizing that my needs may never get met. I realized that I had been fooled and taken advantage of. Even in the ministry, many ministers took advantage of me and came around me for what they could get. Although people say I am hard to approach, they quickly find that I have a soft heart and I am rather gentle. From this, those who drew closer would end up seeing me as a person they could walk all over. It's like I allow people in so easily that they end up taking me over and causing me to bow. This would depress me as I would feel so weak and like there's nothing I could do about it.

This inability to stand up for myself became a pathway to my addictions. Once I accepted someone from my heart, it was almost impossible for me to back off them no matter how much they were hurting me. The biggest ones for me were shame and fear. I had an overwhelming fear of women and being controlled by them which made me to be quite dominating in those relationships. In my early years of dating, I was an extremely insecure and violent person towards my girlfriends and later on my spouse. As I mentioned in the earlier chapters, I had never really loved anyone or experienced true Love in all my life until the birth of my daughter. I used to wonder what was wrong with me. I was cold and full of malice. Being full of fear also meant it was hard for me to confront people properly. If I did, I only exerted anger. I usually avoided confrontations because I never could predict what I was capable of and I was afraid of myself. Some of my Jezebel traits showed up more on the ministry front, these included being harsh at times and controlling when it came to instructions in the delegation of duties.

I would be bewildered by the amazing people around me who seemed to love my fatherly presence but would be so reluctant to execute any instructions given. I did not understand then that most people with Jezebellic traits do not like taking instructions and hate authority! With my short temper, frustrations and anger I became a threatening presence to church and business workers which meant they obeyed more out of fear rather than love. The Jezebel spirit operates primarily through threats and fear. Fear kills intimacy and chases love away. I also used to be a person who makes a 'mountain out of a molehill' and there were times things would dig so deep into my heart and I would explode!

I also started noticing that there were certain patterns with the women in my life. I found them to have strong feminist values which caused them to not respect men and to believe that they were superior to men. Therefore, their goal in life was to change me to be the man who will meet all their needs. I was unaware of what the real issue was. I often reacted with anger at any sign of this. I realized I had unusual responses to them such as fear and self-protection. One key characteristic I noticed is their inability to be open and vulnerable. This applied to nearly all the couples who came to our healing sessions. Their husbands complained of the same things about their wives. On digging deeper, these ladies had deep hatred of men. Most had been sexually abused as children and had vowed to never allow anyone to ever come close to them. Even if they desired to, these early vows were working against them. With such childhood wounding coupled by all the other things that I have and will be sharing in this book, marriages were doomed before they started and were mostly out of balance and loveless. This was the case with my own marriage. This is how the Jezebel/ Ahab dynamic can affect individuals, marriages, families, churches, the market place and entire nations.

Biblical examples of people who had Ahab and Jezebel spirits

Jonathan (1 Samuel 23:17). It's hard to spot it at first but the spirit of Jezebel was all over Jonathan. He figured out that if King Saul killed David then He would be King and if David killed King Saul then he would be second in command. Who gave Jonathan second place? The covenants he made with David were usually on his terms and for his advantage. He was making sure all stops were tied. It was all for selfish motives. The thing is, you cannot be a friend of my enemy. Jezebel does that and it's all deception and it's double mindedness. Jezebel believes she can have loyalties on both sides. This Spirit's goal is to always be next to the person in authority as well as to be worshipped and adored. David knew this about Jonathan as we can see in Psalms 41:6 'and when he comes to see me he speaks falsehood; his heart gathers wickedness to itself when he goes outside he tells it', and he makes reference to this in the entire Psalms 55.

Herod the Great (Matthew 2:1-23). History tells us how wicked and insecure this King was. He was an illegitimate King who murdered his own wives and children. When He heard news of a new born King, he pretended that he also wanted to worship the King while all along his plan was to kill Jesus and the wise men. He wanted to wipe out all competition. The spirit of Jezebel must control anyone of higher authority than her and seeks to kill all genuine prophets. Jesus was the true King and a Prophet.

Absalom (2 Samuel 15:1-12). This level of betrayal was Jezebellic. However, in his case, He did not want to control and manipulate his father by being second in command, he was going for the kill and attempted a Coup and almost succeeded! David on the other hand was Ahabic, very passive so much so that he couldn't see that Absalom was offended for two years, he couldn't see that Ammon was in love with his step sister. He was very unaware of his household affairs.

The Samaritan woman (John 4:7-39). Samaria was the land where the ancient King Ahab and that wicked Queen Jezebel reigned. The land was defiled by the worship of Baal. Jezebel always perverts the true worship of Jehovah! In John 4, Jesus said that He needed to go through Samaria. What was the result of his visit? He restored true worship that had been perverted centuries earlier, he restored a woman with a difficult life and past, she found her true destiny and identity, became a mighty evangelist that brought revival to the region. God showed me that The Samaritan woman was a seductress like Jezebel and she had great hatred in her heart towards men. This led her to finding Ahab's, men who are weak that she could control and manipulate and once she was done with them she spat them out and had no regard for their feelings and emotions.

Herodias (Mark 6:21-29). She was after a man who had power and authority. She would then easily control and manipulate this King. She was jumping from one leader to another because of the shift in power and authority. John the Baptist a true and powerful prophet lost his head due to her sorceries and wicked plots. A true prophet will always expose Jezebel and see right through her, so she got rid of him.

Moses (Exodus 4:10). He had so much self-doubt, a tendency to disqualify himself and was usually plagued with deep fear. These are Ahabic characteristics.

Isaac the promised Son was very passive and his wife Rebekah always had her way. You can see her overpowering influence on her son Jacob. Isaac also willingly lay down on an altar to be sacrificed as a burnt offering. He was also very content to have a wife chosen for him. His father Abraham was also quite independent in the beginning and passive, he easily followed Sarah's decision about having a son with another woman. Jacob was an Ahab; he was controlled by a Jezebellic Uncle Laban. Jacob's experience at uncle's house was his wilderness, and God healed him and he started realising that he was being controlled. He too had picked up controlling ways from his mother but he met his match at uncle Laban's.

I deeply repented of these things and God has really transformed my heart over the years and he has baptized me in His love over this season of the 'dark night of the soul'.

Now that I have come to know how Jezebel and Ahab work, I am adamant about not tolerating these spirits in my environment. I can see that this is how my passion to the calling God has given me is developing, a passion to bring down these spirits. I believe the Lord has given me tools and strategies on how to do so. In all these things, what amazes me most is the absolute genius of our Lord and Savior Jesus Christ. You see, the dynamic I have been describing here is all I have faced with the precious people God sent to me in over a decade of Pastoral ministry largely centered on discipleship, inner healing and deliverance. I often despaired burdened by the great need around me. When God told me years ago that He would heal me as I healed the people He sent my way, I did not understand that everyone who came to us revealed a missing piece of the puzzle to bring healing to my family and I. God sent people from all sorts of racial and ethnic backgrounds over the years, these precious saints were exactly like us. Birds of a feather do flock together! As I have ministered God revealed so much and in this last season, when I had nowhere else to turn to, it was my spiritual children whom God used to restore me. How amazing is that!

I love this scripture;

'But God chose the foolish things of the world to shame the wise; God chose the weak things of the world to shame the strong' (1 Corinthians 1:27)

2. Witchcraft and the Occult

Description

God revealed to me that 'witchcraft is the mankind's rebellion against Him, which leads to seeking alternative gods for comfort, provision and various needs. It is a selfish act that promotes self-reliance and independence. Derek Prince further defines it:

"God's word goes further to identify witchcraft as the 'universal, primeval religion of fallen humanity. When the human race turned from God in rebellion, the power that moved in was witchcraft but certain elements are common to almost all of them. Different people groups practice distinctive forms of witchcraft, but certain elements are common to almost all of them"[1].

Witchcraft is also a work of the flesh as listed in Galatians 5:19-21 'idolatry, sorcery….'

The spirit of Jezebel operates through witchcraft to tamper with our God-given destiny and derail us from God's purpose so that our lives are surrendered to her will. In my case there has been no one in my immediate family who practiced witchcraft, and as a matter of fact, it was disregarded and deemed ancient and irrelevant.

When growing up I always heard stories about my grandfather who was a witchdoctor. Yet, through my healing sessions God began to reveal that there were high levels of witchcraft in my generational background, going back at least 10 generations. We learned that the covenants made by my ancestors for perversion and money were done through satanic rituals that involved various abuses. This was done in quest for solutions to relational, marital and other problems they were facing in life. In those days, the witchdoctor was seen as the 'medicine man', a traditional term used for a healer or spiritual healer. The 'medicine man' was one who resolved all the problems of those around him. He was like their counsellor, doctor and refuge.

Effects

As an adult I questioned why there were so many prevalent problems, devastation, chaos and brokenness around me. These were

---

1   The Teaching Legacy of Derek Prince; The Seeking Of Control, Volume XIV issue3, 1998

the signs of witchcraft that were disregarded in my life, yet we barely recognized it. I knew I loved God, but I could not understand why even though I was genuine, I still lived a life full of limitations and great spiritual torment. Though I was a Pastor, I found that these witchcraft mantles placed limitations on my level of intimacy with God. I was blinded from knowing my identity and purpose in Christ and the manifestation of the Holy Spirit was shut down in my life.

I also experienced great inconsistences in Christian life. Whilst I believe that my prayer life and the reading of God's word were through the flow of the Holy Spirit, I could not really say I knew Him. Witchcraft opened doors to the enemy to sabotage the gifts God had given me. Where I was called naturally to be strong, I seemed to be weak. For example, even as a Pastor I really struggled with the things of the Spirit, it was as though my spiritual antennas were blocked. I could hardly sense the Spirit's movement, it was very difficult to receive the baptism of the Holy Spirit and operate in the gifts of the Spirit. Furthermore, my prophetic visions were completely closed down and I could not hear the voice of God. But God revealed that this was all the doing of the enemy to hinder me in an area that was so crucial for my destiny. I discovered that if I had served the enemy, these things would have worked. At the time I did not know all these things and I just used to feel so unworthy as a leader of God's people.

Witchcraft powers are like magnets; they cause you to be attracted to things of that nature. Where there is witchcraft in your background, your life has already been programmed to follow a particular way. Satan gives a destiny different from what God has for you. He places traps that cause trauma, bitterness and confusion to destroy your life and bring havoc into the lives of others. If your life is not aligned to God's will, Satan uses every access point to destroy you and those around you. Even as a Christian, I found myself with these struggles. I have discovered that you attract like-minded people and this was true of the relationships I formed. Witchcraft roots or foundations can even lead you to church groups that are spiritually dangerous or that have cultic tendencies. These roots also placed a curiosity in me which was attracted to horror movies and Satanism whilst at High School. Through healing sessions, God revealed that this was due to witchcraft roots in my life.

Learned and discovered

Surprisingly, in the midst of these limitations, God used me to set other people free. As a pastor of a deliverance ministry this was expected of me. When God began to expose the witchcraft in my life, I realised how crucial this was to my breakthrough and that a lot of my limitations in ministry had to do with witchcraft covenants initiated by my ancestors. My grandfather had destined me to follow in his footsteps as he was a witchdoctor and I was next in line destined to take the witchcraft mantle, so that I continue witchcraft in the family line. God revealed that there was a witchcraft mantle upon my life. This began to explain the things I experienced especially at High School. These included a fascination with occult books and being targeted for recruitment by devil worshippers. The biggest issue was the extreme instability in my Christian walk; one minute I was so fervently in love with the Lord and the next minute I was malicious, angry and in deep sin.

As a result I developed a philosophy that if I was going to hell I would have a ball and go to hell. I was disgusted in myself with these extremities, so much so that I thought why do God and end up in hell? But for some reason I could not walk away from doing God. I was always asking, what is wrong with me? All this had a severe impact on me. I had severe depression and unexplainable illnesses and I felt afraid for my life. I was forced to drop out of school and I fled Kenya.

Impact

Through the process of prophetic healing and deliverance, all these things were exposed. I discovered that what I perceived as the problem was only 10% of the actual problem. It felt like looking at an iceberg, not realising that beneath the water the iceberg is 10 times as big. God led me through systematic prayers, breaking generational witchcraft curses, witchcraft covenants and bringing healing to my heart. Through the prayers, generational hindrances have fallen off. I am no longer walking in the shadows of those generational curses. I am now walking in the newness of life. I have learned how to be myself and now feel free as compared to when I felt trapped and controlled. I felt like the man who God had called me to be was unleashed, leaving me to feel safe and secure in my identity. I could feel my heart come alive and begin to beat again. I have learned how to express my heart more and I have become a genuinely happier man. I am also able to walk in the newness of personality. I was able to come out of great depression and shame. I began to discover the gifts and talents God had placed in me all along. God has unlocked the fullness of my prophetic gifting by releasing greater insight and accuracy.

3. Sexual perversion

Description:

In the Bible, sexual perversion is used to define a deviation from righteousness in sexual behavior (Leviticus18:23; Romans 1:27; Ephesians 4:19; Colossians 3:5). Sex is a gift God gave man within the context of marriage. Sexual perversion, on the other hand, is influenced by the enemy and it breaks God's covenant, and brings pain and damage to families and individuals.

Effects

On 3 November 1995, I attended my first deliverance session accompanied by my Mum. As I confessed all my sins, and my Mum later commented "you know son you always argue with me when I say that mothers really know their children, let me tell you something, when you were an infant, you used to play with your genitals so much that I became so worried. I tried to tell your Dad, and he would say, 'no that is how boys are, leave him alone'. But now that I have heard this confession, I know I was right."

Years later, I learned that it was not uncommon for an infant to turn to their genitals seeking comfort. It felt like a relief when I learned others had similar experiences as mine. This brought answers for me. Another thing that has plagued me is this long life fascination with female genitalia. I remember at five years old, when female children would come over to our house, I would be fascinated to see their genitals whilst their nappies were being changed. Since that time as I grew up I knew that something was 'a little off'. I began to be addicted to masturbation and pornography from the age of about 10. I remember always having voyeuristic tendencies. I started being aware that this is not right or acceptable behavior, and so I had this intense shame that affected my identity and I carried this secrecy around that lead me to being consumed with feelings of worthlessness.

Learned and discovered

I have now come to know that this condition is called intimacy disorder. I have learned that this is usually a sign of deep loneliness, lack of nurture and connection. This means that the inability to be intimate is due to a misguided understanding that intimacy is in actual fact sex. So sex becomes a primary source of connection and not real intimacy that requires knowing each other from the heart. If intimacy is absent in marriage where it is most desired then usually it is because the couple has this intimacy disorder and they are probably addicted to sex. If there are instances of abuse and trauma in one's life, it can shatter their ability to be intimate as their sense of worth and their sense of trust is lost. This can be seen through addictions such as pornography.

Throughout my life, I have been sexually addicted in various forms. The worst thing is the shame it brings and the fear of discovery. Sexual addictions always come with a sense of covering up, not to let others know what is going on, leading to shame. We have learned that sexual perversion, witchcraft and poverty are connected and that one cannot stand alone. This is why there is a large amount of these traits in many lives. Such generational patterns can be so deep rooted in our lives. They cause deep pain, trauma and hindrances. I discovered that the enemy only needs a small leeway and from there he can turn a seemingly 'innocent' act into a perverted act leading to problems in the lives of people and children. This is how Jezebel latches on and begins to control so that there is a contin- uation of sin and oppression.

God has shown me that He is the solution, He is the only one who can meet this deep longing and need we have deep inside of us. Through prophetic inner healing and deliverance, God revealed the causes or roots behind my struggles. For me, it is almost as though all I had to do was to be born in a certain family line where these things were prevalent. God took my healing team into the spirit through visions into those ancient places where my ancestors had made lots of covenants such as witchcraft, sexual perversion and money covenants. He showed me that sexual acts were required when people sought particular favours from witchdoctors. The Lord revealed to us that my forefathers would seek witchdoctors to help solve their sexual inadequacies; however, this caused the men to have very high sex drives and to be promiscuous and this is believed to be the root of polygamy in families generally as they would feel deeply unsatisfied with their wives. There was a belief that sex had the power and was a tool to control women, so that they never leave them. Many people think that once they are married their problems are sorted, but in actual fact, through the open doors from witchcraft covenants, the problems still persist.

One example that I want to give is when we were asking Jesus to reveal more roots for sexual perversion; we entered into a prophetic vision where we saw a great grandfather from six generations ago. He was in some sort of ritual with a witchdoctor and they were dedicating the family to Satan. We saw all the men in my family in chains and they were like slaves, all helpless when it came to lust, pornography and masturbation. This was something set in stone for the men to fall in the same sexual sins; it was a generational pattern. We were able to then renounce, repent and break these things in the name of Jesus. Jesus showed me in the same prayer ministry session that I was abused sexually as a child under five years old on three separate occasions by maids. Additionally, I was exposed to a lot of female nudity at around the same time. From these incidences images of female body parts were burned into my subconscious. I never remembered these incidences and I remember crying so much to God wondering why I had all these struggles all my life not knowing that it was from things these women made me do. It explained my hatred of women and need to punish them.

I also learnt that lust came from my early childhood porn consumption. This made me have a strong desire to do what I had seen in pornographic images. I also had vague memories of me and other boys touching each other during my early teenage years. God clarified this and I saw there was unwanted touching of my private parts from men in my childhood. This was one of the root causes of my difficulties to relate to men; I have always felt safer in the company of women even though there has always been a love and hate relationship with them. These revelations and subsequent ministrations have brought profound healing that I never thought was possible. This is what Jesus can do.

Generally when a child is born, certain activities, behaviours or rituals undertaken can trigger the evil generational traits of sexual perversion. We have seen this in my example above. This results in serious levels of bondage and curses that seem impossible to break and are seriously overpowering for many throughout their lives. Even as a Christian, it is difficult to break away from these things because their roots had been grown and accumulated through generations. This is one area that the Body of Christ is really battling with.

I have come to understand by revelation the way the spirit of sexual perversion works. Sexual perversion is really a club or group of sexual demons. These all work together and cannot be isolated one from another. Sexual demons include lust, fornication, adultery, oral sex, anal sex, voyeurism, nudity, uncleanness, rape, incubus, succubus, spiritual husbands and wives, incest, sexual abuse, homosexuality, bestiality, pedophilia and the like. Once the door of sexual perversion opens up, any one of these traits can easily manifest in an individual. It is usually just circumstantial and down to what one is exposed to. It is important to recognize that they are all connected. Some signs can help you identify that the currency of sexual perversion is in operation in your life. These include fantasies, the type of pornography that one is drawn to, lust and what one finds fascinating.

However, the greatest identifier is the laws of judgment as given in Deuteronomy 5:16; Matthew 7:1-2; Romans 2:1-2; Hebrews 12:15. Whose sin do you judge the most? Have you ever wondered why so many church leaders are falling in all forms of sexual sin? Yet we leaders at the same time come down so hard on those who sin in similar ways. All sin is sin, even though human beings may judge some sin more severely. We have often castigated people who cannot even change without love, acceptance, nurture and support. We are good at leaving our wounded on the battlefield because often we have not known how to help.

The deeper the sexual perversion, the more likely the person feels lonely, unloved, unaccepted and rejected. By the Grace of God, we are seeing the Lord touching sexually addicted people whatever their background. The roots are the same, the remedy is the same. The laws of judgment as I mentioned earlier suggests that we attract who we are and we judge strictly what we deny in ourselves but see it in others. Usually God's grace covers us and we may not manifest some behaviours. When we operate in judging and condemning others who sin differently from us, we are actually taking God's grace and attributing it as our character. This is pride and it always precedes a fall (Proverbs 16:18; James 4:6). Let us minister with grace and in vulnerability as it is the most effective way to help those who are struggling, not with self-righteousness. If we face our own past and our own struggles, we will be able to accept others and see that God is willing to heal and redeem the lost and the broken. Nothing is impossible with God and no one is beyond His reach.

One more thing the Lord showed me is that deep perversion reveals deep witchcraft and occultism in the generations if not in the present life. Severe money issues have roots in the occult and sexual perversion too. These all operate under the marine kingdom of darkness; under the principality of Jezebel.

Being oppressed by sexual perversion can feel like operating under a drug. One can start facing side effects such as deep depression, self-hatred, fear and paranoia. It drags us into a place where we feel powerless and unable to fight it, as these forces come on so strong no matter how wrong it is we may feel unable to defend ourselves against this spirit. The shame that it brings can cause us to experience withdrawal and isolation. We can feel as though we have lost a part of ourselves when it comes to committing sexually perverted acts but as we know it starts with thoughts, we can feel as though we have been defiled by our own thoughts but the other end of the spectrum looks like complete desire. We can feel like there is something so wrong that no one could ever love or accept someone like us.

Other effects of sexual perversion are evident in all outward relationships, as it can shut down all forms of intimacy. Upwardly, it can cause great limitations in our relationship with God, not because we are rejected but because our shame and self-hatred shuns us and this limit our relationship with God. It also continues down the generations and so when we commit sexual perversion we are planting a seed in the lives of our future generations.

God has shown us that what we need is to be intimate with Him. This is all about connection, relationship, fellowship, trust, safety, freedom, acceptance and unconditional love. Without this, Satan uses addictions to give us a false sense of intimacy. These addictions replace God and become idols, where we go to get fed or to draw comfort and get our needs met, yet only God's Spirit can truly satisfy us (Jeremiah 2:13).

For instance, I battled with lust so much that it got to a point where I realised that no matter how attractive and beautiful a woman was, she could not satisfy me. With sexual addiction, we come to a point where we end up accumulating several partners, until it becomes an ongoing cycle. This traps us in shame and cycles of defeat, withdrawal, self-hatred, and developing a need to punish the women that we love, even though we may want to be around them. All these things damage our relationships, our identities and that sense of worth.

Satan gives us false intimacies as an alternative to intimacy with the Lord.

How do we develop intimacy with God? God loves us and understands what we go through. God is the solution, it is God we need, He is such an understanding God, He wants to touch our lives. There are many things we are blaming ourselves for that we just simply cannot overcome on our own. God knows and sees us. God has called us. As a matter of fact, the area you are most attacked could be an indication that this is the very area that you are called to and that your redemptive gifts will manifest the most. You may be in the place where there are so many contradictions, so that even if someone came and gave you a word that God would use you to help people to break out from certain habits, it will be difficult for you to accept it. This is because those bad habits might have been the greatest struggle for you also. Rest assured that there is hope. If God can heal me of my stuff and of my addictions, certainly he can heal you as well. You just need the right set of tools, just to know what to do and most certainly He will heal you. Allow God to show you people who can help and God will completely deliver you, and you will be a completely different person from who you are right now.

Impact

My worst struggle has been in the area of sexual perversion; for a long time the enemy made me believe that I was the only one who struggled like this. I was desperate and it took a long time to get to a place where I could be healed. I have come to understand that I needed to identify with the people who I was called to reach out to, so that there is full compassion from a place of understanding and not from a place of judgement. It started from desperation to overcome and wanting to defeat my problems, wanting to be changed. We also need to encounter the truth; we need a truthful perspective of the problem. If you do not understand what your problem is, it is difficult to overcome it. The Bible says that 'it is the truth that sets us free' (John 8:32); because where there is no truth, there are lies and lies keep us in bondage. The truth definitely set me free as it made me realise the depth of my problem. There were lots of lies I believed about myself, about God and the people around me. An encounter with the truth is really important. The truth is both in the written Word of God, which needs to be known, and in encoun- tering Jesus Christ Himself. Jesus says that, "I am the way, the truth and the life" (John 14:6). We need to have an encounter with Jesus Christ which is a bit more than an intellectual understanding of Him. Over the years God has helped us to have some tools and they have helped us to deal with these things. Through the prophetic and hearing God's voice, we are able to ask the Lord to guide us and lead us into the areas where some of these problems are. God revealed many things like how I had been programmed to think and act in a certain way and these things strengthened the bondage; so it was overpowering me, and I found myself in places where I felt victimised, and felt my problems had an unfair advantage over me. I found that the various tools of inner healing were able to help me tackle and overcome these challenges.

4. Poverty

Description:

Poverty is a mindset which is perpetuated and that operates from the spirit of Mammon. Individuals with poverty mindsets are slaves to Mammon and they firmly believe they will always lack. This produces a great fear of money. Those with poverty mindsets also never think of ways of how to receive money or how to increase their money. Poverty mindsets affect all areas of their life because their fear of money will affect the job they have or aim to reach for and their lifestyle.

"No one can serve two masters. For either he will hate the one, and love the other; or else he will hold to the one and despise the other. You cannot serve God and Mammon" The Bible defines Mammon as the spirit behind money. (Mathew 6:24)

We mentioned that Mammon is one of the biggest principalities that Satan uses. When you are tied down to the spirit of Mammon, you are tied to poverty. People with a poverty mindset may be wealthy but still spend money as if they were poor. Mammon replaces faith and it initiates fear and control towards money. It is a spirit that causes financial error and financial mismanagement. People bound by this spirit cannot sow their money in the right places and their money cannot partner with God's kingdom.

Effects

Poverty manifests in various forms. For some people, they find it difficult to give; they hold on to money or save a lot not because of any godly principles but because of the fear of not having. For others they even spend when they don't have much. Poverty can manifest in two extremes: spending less or overspending. Others can be extremely stingy, withholding tithes and offering, completely controlling the money they have. This spirit is behind many money- related habits including stealing, not working hard, feelings of financial inadequacy, not investing or not taking financial risks etc. Poverty weighs us down completely.

It causes us to be subjected to money and allow money problems to consume us. In my case, I tend to mismanage my money; I either spend it on others or make unwise decisions. I find that my priorities can be distorted which leads to unproductive decisions regarding money. This has also affected my ministry. I always felt like there was a lot of robbery and a sense of being defrauded, where I would never receive what was due to me. People were always reluctant to give back to the church and I. I could see the irregularities and how unusual this was.

Having a poverty mind-set meant that I tolerated so many things and I became passive when it came to receiving financial support from the ministry. I felt guilty to receive from people and I thought because I was serving God, He would reward me at some point in time. Being bound by poverty has brought a lot of shame in my life. People have looked down on me as I have had to live on a very minimal income. It has been such a struggle my whole life. I cannot truly say apart from my childhood life, that I have lived comfortably in this area. My family has suffered the most.

Learned and discovered:

God started revealing how this poverty mind-set is entrenched in me and how this affected me as well as why it was so difficult financially.

There were so many generational curses over money in my family. Through prophetic ministry, God showed me that some ancestors of mine made money covenants in witchcraft and this held us bound as in we could not produce harvests, we could not generate wealth the way God wanted us to and not really reach our full potential in life. Nothing good ever comes out of seeking help from the enemy, like my ancestors did, instead of the only capable God. The enemy comes to steal, kill and destroy. When we partner with the enemy in areas like occult involvement, we are giving him access into our lives and families for generations (Leviticus 26:39; Deuteronomy 5:8-10).

This is the reality I had lived in for a long time and yet it has been such a contradiction compared to what God has said over my future. I have had prophecies saying that the reasons why jobs did not work for me was because I was called to be an entrepreneur, one who raises others into business, help businesses be established and that God would use me for the transference of wealth into the Kingdom. This is a really big calling upon my life. The Lord said to me "son I have called you to be a business-man of business-men, a leader of leaders and a pastor of pastors". My apostolic calling is both in the market place and in the Church.

On the contrary, my life has not shown any of these prophesied signs to date and I used to wonder why. This is yet another contra- diction in my life. God has been advising me that the only way to reverse the evil done in this area is through intense generosity.

He said "Son I want you to hear my voice in this area. I will show you how best to give money away as I know you love to seek knowledge and have bought many books but even in this let Me show you how to do it and when to do it. Son, you are also not obliged to give to everyone, I love your heart of generosity and compassion but involve me son'. He revealed that the spirit of Mammon influences me to believe that everything is profitable, which could be true for all of us, but He said be careful dear not everything that looks spiritual is necessarily for you. It is about setting priorities and discerning what needs to be spent on but most importantly involving God in all money-making decisions

Impact

As a result of this revelation and seeking healing, I have seen a tremendous change in this area of my life. God has exerted much boldness in me to start various projects; the first one is the making of this book. God has caused me to raise entrepreneurs around me whom I now manage and also I am about to venture into being a life coach. I feel as if he has installed a whole new perspective in this area, I am starting afresh with God. There is so much hope now. For example, I have realised that I am talented in organising events especially church events and conferences. To date, I have organised and hosted over 40 conferences in the period of 5 years. With God's leading, we are now setting up an events management company which is a part of a business calling on my life which God has revealed. He promises me glory in my finances and that though it seems shameful, He will cause it all to shine. Now as I partner with God, I understand that He is bringing me into Kingdom wealth and He is raising me up as a business man just as he intended. There are many business ideas He has given me that I am looking forward to execute.

5. *Fear*

Description:

Fear is the paralysis of faith. It is also the lack of affirmation and the opposite of love. Fear is simply faith in the Devil. One day, God showed that fear had absolutely paralysed me.

"There is no fear in love; but perfect love casts out fear, because fear involves punishment, and the one who fears is not perfected in love" (1 John 4:18)

The fact that you are bound by fear is an indication that you lack love in your life. In the book of Deuteronomy 1:21 and Isaiah 41:10, God is always encouraging us not to fear, because he knows it can limit us. Interestingly there are 365 'fear nots' in the Bible.

Effects

Unfortunately, fear is something that has always been in my life. It was like a huge tree that started off as a small seed and as I grew older the more and more fear grew in me. Further traumatic events kept adding to it. The roots were so deep that only God could reveal them. For instance, during pregnancy, my Mother faced various near death situations. Whatever emotions she was going through, I experienced them too as a baby in her womb. This is how the spirit of death entered into my life. I was told that my birth was complicated. It was a traumatic forceps delivery where the doctors had to consider either losing the baby or saving mum. I came out miraculously with severe forceps injuries to my head. As a child, I was constantly sick; always in hospital, no wonder I always had this fear of living. I used to have death wishes; I never really wanted to live. The whole environment of my childhood had something to do with danger, insecurity and some kind of instability. We were used to thieves and robbers attempting to break into our childhood home nearly every week. I had a big fear of authority, which can be traced back to my African family structure.

I was really fearful of everything. I remember in school I would not participate and would do the very best to avoid debates and public speaking. I had the fear of people and a fear of failure, making it difficult for me to step out into things. I was just the person who would hide away in the background. Plus, I attended a boarding school where pupils were severely beaten by teachers. It was a very abusive learning environment.

Fear was something that actually tormented and controlled me most of my life. As mentioned earlier, I was fearful of women. This immense fear appeared even with my own wife. Whenever conflicts arose with her, I would get this really uncomfortable sensation in my stomach, it felt like a storm and I would instantly have stomach runs.

Fear has robbed me of joy and satisfaction. The Bible says that you attract what you fear (Job 3:25); Fear can limit your whole life. Have you noticed the Bible constantly says 'do not fear'?

There were certain things I could not do because of perfectionism and passivity. These are also forms of fear. I also had great fear of rejection and abandonment. I used to have a need to be accepted and that meant that I was a people pleaser. Fear has been a massive thing that has been really limiting me even as a Minister of the Gospel. There have been many opportunities I have put off or missed, and as a result I have disappointed many people just because of fear. The unfortunate encounter with moral failure further opened another wide door of fear in my life. I became fearful of everything and found there was an alter of self-protection. I became suspicious, angry, upset, agitated, and I felt unsure as to whether I wanted friends or not. Fear is False Evidence Appearing Real, it is an illusion that the enemy creates. On the other hand, faith actually hopes in a futuristic reality; which is a concept from God.

Learned and discovered

I discovered that there was generational fear. My parents lived during the times of the struggle of independence in Kenya. Family members died in this war and it was a time of great insecurity. Before the time of independence, my Kikuyu tribe would be constantly at war with the neighbouring Maasai tribe. Many atrocities were done during these tribal wars. I also know that my immediate paternal grandfather was a soldier for the British army in the 1st World War of 1914-1918. There was a lot of generational trauma and pain carried down our family DNA (Deoxyribonucleic acid).

Impact

God started to strip off the layers of fear in my life as He uncovered where fear had originated from in my family. I was able to see things for what they actually were and I began to go through healing from the bondage of fear. He took me back to the womb to where I first encountered fear and how that experience had created a fear of living. That explained a lot of the suicidal struggles I faced in my life even as a youth. He explored the many different types of fear and showed me how it had operated in my life. God began to expose how the spirit of Jezebel uses fear. Satan primarily uses fear to rule and to reign; his whole kingdom operates on fear. It is a very satanic thing in its core. During the healing sessions, God began to visit the various traumatic experiences of my life and showed us the genera- tional roots they had stemmed from. God showed me how to stand up for myself, believe in myself and build healthy boundaries.

God gave me a strategy on how to manage my fears, He told me "whenever you feel fearful, go into my Word or ask me what the truth is. Then give me your fears". Earlier on, we mentioned that when we are bound by fear it is an indication of the lack of love.

God revealed that one of the most powerful weapons against fear is the revelation of the Father's love. Love dissipates fear. I have more recently come into a fuller revelation of fear in my life as I was writing this book. I nearly gave up as it really plagued me. I now know that this is the one area that the enemy uses most to stop me from accomplishing my assignments and fully stepping in to the opportunities that God brings my way. I realized that I was afraid of success! This is one stone I am yet to fully conquer but I am doing it afraid. God also said that it is important that we know our identity in Christ. I have learned to know the Father's love, which at least now helps to keep fear away, only His love can dissipate my fears. Father God also said it is important to know who I am as in my true identity in God. That is what I want to address next.

Identity

Identity is the foundation of who you are on this earth. It is the role of a father to install identity into a child. Thus, the lack of identity can be a result of not having a father in our lives or having an emotionally absent father. Knowing who you are (your identity), is vital because it shapes your sense of value and worth. I grew up not really loving myself or my life because no one affirmed who I was. My identity came from illegitimacy, sexual perversion, insecurity and all the things we have been addressing throughout this book. Coming from a background like this, the process of knowing who you are becomes difficult. The enemy actually tormented me through this by making me feel shameful about my sins. I had self-disgust and self-hatred. These feelings would attach themselves to my identity, thus creating a hold for Jezebel to keep me in bondage by constantly speaking negative words pertaining to my identity.

I remember in one healing session, we saw the spirit of Jezebel torturing a fear alter personality, she had tied down this alter and was feeding him with lies to stop him from believing in himself. I can undoubtedly say that fear has held me back in ministry and it is because Jezebel has constantly reminded me of my failures. Knowing who you are will diminish or decrease the influence of Jezebel in your life. Jesus defeated Jezebel because He knew his true identity, whenever she came to accuse or twist the truth through the religious leaders of his day, Jesus declared who He was. (Matthew 9:2-6; John 14:30).

I have come to find out that without identity you cannot be intimate with the God head – Father, Son and Holy Spirit. Identity is a founda- tional structure that needs to be in place in order to fulfil destiny or to walk in Sonship and to defeat Jezebel. Jezebel uses our identities because she knows that if she holds that part of you, you cannot be fully transformed into a true Son, a son is one who knows himself. Many faithful believers are trying their best to live according to the word of God through applying Godly principles, yet there is a lack of deep personal fulfilment because they are not true sons (John 5:39). Many are very successful; nevertheless they lack intimacy. As a result they end up ignoring many things in their lives, whilst others have been sweeping those things under the carpet. The problem is a global one.

We have an unknown enemy that we have not learnt to discern properly. This limits true spiritual intimacy as Jesus demonstrated it. As mentioned, Jesus was the only one who defeated Jezebel, even John the Baptist who was 'the greatest of all born of women' (Luke 7:28) lost his head to a Jezebellic-fuelled set-up. Jezebel killed him because he proclaimed the Messiah. Jezebel aims to erase any trace of Christ. However, Jesus went on to say that, 'the least in the kingdom of God was greater than he'. What we need to understand is that, knowing who we are combined with spiritual intimacy powerfully impacts our relationships with God and man. God uses the wilderness season to unveil our true identity in him. This process can be painful leaving us feeling bare and empty, but that is because He just wants us to know who we are.

The way that God brought restoration for me was through extravagant love and unconditional acceptance, healing, identity and intimacy. When you do not know who you are you cannot really love yourself or give yourself to anyone, either God or man. Intimacy becomes impossible. God gave me a new identity and a new nickname to match. He said my identity was like gold and He gave me the name 'Golden Boy'. He said this name represents my prominence on this earth and my kingship. He revealed to me that my identity was perfect and precious and I was to proclaim it over myself daily. The Lord said that I was a king, a conqueror, a defender and an achiever. I am a leader, one who redeems, one who overcomes and a champion. The Lord spoke His truth to me that my identity was true and pure. The Lord spoke over my life over and over again declaring that I am pure, that I belonged and that I was accepted.

Subsequently, I was able to love and accept myself, I felt anew. Jezebel will from time to time prey on our identities but we must remember God's word. I am a Son to God and He is teaching me that this is enough and I have learned to be content in this. God wants you to know that you are His child and that He is your Father. Sonship is your identity.

The fivefold ministry

Jesus left his children with a gift; this is known as the fivefold ministry which consists of Apostles, Prophets, Evangelists, Pastors and Teachers (Ephesians 4:11-12). Jesus' heart for fivefold was to equip the saints so that they reach their God-given destinies. Many do not know that different callings carry certain assignments, though they are not absolute, but on a larger scale you can see how they work for the kingdom. Jesus intended for them to work in unity to bring down the kingdom of darkness. The pastor is a gift for the people, to take care of their needs and to look after them; teachers are meant to teach God's principles; and the evangelist pulls people from the kingdom of darkness into the kingdom of light, showing them that darkness is not a good place to be in; the prophet directs, exhorts and corrects the saints whilst also searching out the Rhema word (spoken or revealed word) of God for the church. The apostle makes the way for others; he clears the air and brings in the culture of heaven. The biggest hindrance coming against the fivefold from working together is Jezebel. She blinds the church with denomina- tional and cultural differences hindering unity. The body of Christ needs to recognize that all callings are needed to keep Jezebel defeated in the nations.

Jezebel and the Apostolic

From what I have come to know God has placed apostles at a higher level and has given them difficult assignments. This is not disregarding the other callings in the fivefold. There is a significance about Apostles that shines through and is clearly demonstrated in their ministries. From a biblical point of view, it is clear that they are mainly called to bring down principalities and demons; they are called to the dark world and Satan tends to oppress them because of their assignments. If Satan can destroy an apostle in a town, city or nation, then he has built his own kingdom. Apostles are called to spend time with the Father.

"So the twelve summoned the congregation of the disciples and said, "It is not desirable for us to neglect the word of God in order to serve tables." (Acts 6:2)

Apostles are prone to strive; they have the worst attacks from the enemy especially aimed at their identities. One thing that I have noticed is that Jezebel blinded me so much from knowing who I am in Christ; I would not have known that I was an apostle called to do this assignment by The Lord to bring down principalities because of how Jezebel had tarnished my identity through fear and shame. Some biblical apostles with similar assignments are Moses and Nehemiah. Moses' calling clearly seems to be an apostolic one; God calls him to deliver people from what metaphorically appears to be a principality called Pharaoh. (Exodus 6:6). Apostles are looked down on and discredited by Jezebel; Nehemiah was a victim of this. She aimed to take away his authority by destroying his reputation. Jezebel tormented him only through words using Sanballat and Tobias (Nehemiah 6:12-13).

Everyday attacks

From time to time, I may face some Jezebelic set-ups; this is where she whispers negativity in your ears and brings attacks that make you feel worthless. These attacks come in the form of depression, fear, anxiety, frustration, feelings of worthlessness and feelings of failure. She brought these everyday emotions to tear me down. They are designed to turn my eyes away from the bigger picture, but through healing sessions I am able to defeat the lies that she feeds me by receiving the truth of Christ.

As the injured soldier lays in bed wishing the doctor would give them something to nurse the pain. He begins to realise that his pain was beyond the physical. His pain was deep within, the ache is unbearable, the wounds are beyond repair. His heart is broken; the trauma from rejection constantly taunts him. The disgust towards the abuse he experienced causes him to hate himself. The soldier needed one touch from God!! From a past of pain and anguish.

Chapter 5

Lessons learned

Proverbs 3:3-6 NIV
Let love and faithfulness never leave you; bind them around
your neck, write them on the tablet of your heart. Then you
will win favour and a good name in the sight of God and man.
Trust in the Lord with all your heart and lean not on your own
understanding; in all your ways submit to him, and he will make
your paths straight.

'Son all you have learned in this season is for a purpose you are not only making a way for yourself but also for generations to come, your immediate and extended family. Those you lead and are called to impact. All has not been wasted instead it's been invested into a brighter future. Your pain will benefit others after you, so son do not give up, look at the lessons I am showing you and tell them to others. I want to show them my glory through your life. Will you allow me?'

[Seer Journal entry, 2014]

Going through such a Wilderness was essential for me as I learned lessons useful to help others navigate their way out of their own Wilderness seasons. I encourage you to endure, knowing that the gains are considerable. Looking at the lessons and how positive they are, I believe my Wilderness season was ordained by God. He really anoints us to do well. The most significant lesson I have learned is to depend only upon God and not people, objects, or other sources. It has to be Him, it will not work any other way. I have also learned to be fully submissive to God's instructions; not to move until He speaks. Other things I have learned include encountering God's extravagant love, intimacy with God, hearing the voice of God, the power of the prophetic and seer realms, creating healthy relational boundaries within a Kingdom culture and so much more.

Experiencing God's love

As I mentioned earlier in this book, I grew up feeling unloved and God has revealed many things about this which I have already discussed in other chapters. Of all the lessons that I have learned, in my opinion, experiencing God's love is the most important one. We know all the scriptures about love and often we use them as a stick to beat each other up when we feel we are not as loved as we feel we ought to be. Often the expectation is on demanding that others love us and not necessarily that we give or love unconditionally. The truth is, many of us are so broken and have never really experienced true love. Our parents could only do the best they could and they offered their best in most cases. God is love (1 John 4:8) and we are born for love and by love. Love is an essential ingredient and we cannot function wholesomely without it. God's love is unconditional and the first thing He did with me was to pour His love into me unreservedly and continuously. God brought an awesome company of people around me to pour in love into my life. He said He was showing me how much He loves me through them. I became more alive, finding new hope.

Brothers and sisters, love is the secret to resurrection. I realised that knowing I was loved was not the same as experiencing and receiving the love. We all have different love languages namely; touch, gifts, quality time, acts of service and words of affirmation[1]. This time God packaged it just for me. I learned in this season that God's love can be supernaturally experienced and imparted. I think this was God's priority during this season. He has shown me great love.

The lack of love leads to sin, as we are left looking for ways to fill up the void within us. Such void produces dependency and co-dependency in relationships, forcing us to look outside for that void to be filled up. These are unhealthy ways of trying to gain love from people instead of God. We need a Godly balance of receiving love both from humans and God otherwise when we have not experienced this love at a human level, we find it difficult to receive directly from God.

1   The Five Love Languages, Gary D. Chapman, Northfield Publishing, 2010

When one has not experienced love in a way that is uniquely expressed to them, their heart is usually shut down, making it hard to have heartfelt intimate relationships. This is where the enemy introduces false comforts and false intimacy through various addictions, fantasies and idolatry. I started to be restored as I began to experience God's love. I now know that people need to know they are loved. This has to be genuine and as people begin to feel accepted and loved, fear really dissipates. It becomes so much easier for them to believe in themselves, in God's love and to become free. It also causes hope to arise in their heart.

Seeing the Mercies of God

I have come to know the love and mercies of God in my Wilderness season because I have seen His forgiveness and His Grace. Mercy is different to grace because it expresses withheld punishment. In other words, God pardons us from the punishment we deserve. Grace is unmerited favour where God gives us what we do not deserve. It is what we receive from God beyond the mercy He shows us (Rom 3:24).

God spoke and said to me:

> 'Son I am showing you all this because you will have mercy on other leaders who have fallen... Where the Kingdom has thrown them out, shunned them and put a lot of shame on them; you will bring them back and build them up, trust them and love them because I have loved you and have had mercy on you. I have not removed anything from you. I have not removed your name, it is still written in my book of life. Your anointing is still there, your calling still stands and your destiny still stands. I have not removed anything from you.'

These words came to me from the Living God in my 'dark night of the soul' and powerfully ministered to my heart. I sensed God was giving me the keys to help the Kingdom resurrect or restore fallen church leaders. Unlike having a Wilderness season where the body of Christ fails to help, God wants church leaders to be looked after. This is all His mercy and grace. Mercy like love is so important in this hour. The mercy I have received in this season will help me teach the church how to treat, love, trust and have mercy on the fallen and those who have similar issues. The majority of church leaders do not really understand why they find themselves in sinful patterns and predicaments. Let us realise that when we fall short of God's glory His love and mercy are always available. For me, I have been amazed at how much mercy he has shown me. His solutions are always love and mercy.

Psalm 103:8-10 NIV

The Lord is merciful and gracious, slow to anger and plenteous in mercy and loving-kindness. He will not always chide or be contending, neither will He keep His anger forever or hold a grudge. He has not dealt with us after our sins nor rewarded us according to our iniquities.

Hearing God's Voice

Deuteronomy 5:24 says that 'We have heard His Voice…. We have seen this day that God speaks with man.' Spiritual communication or intimacy has also been one of the most important aspects of my whole experience. Not only is communion God's deepest desire, I learned that only God's voice could save me from all I went through. God wants us to hear His voice, He will teach us to hear him even in the most difficult moments. The Bible also teaches that when we listen and obey His voice we will encounter many blessings (Deuteronomy 28:1-14). His voice has guided me through my Wilderness season. It would have been a disaster, without hearing from Him. God is not quiet in the 'dark seasons of our lives'. God spoke to me all the way through my 'dark night of the soul' as I have been illustrating elsewhere. John 10:27 states, "my sheep hear my voice, I know them and they follow me". This Scripture sets no time limit; it just says we can hear Him. His voice has delivered me from the hands of the enemy many times. His voice has also delivered me from following rational conclusions. Scriptures tell us that "there is a way that seems right to a man but its end is death" (Proverbs 14:12).

I learned to not rely on my own human understanding in my Wilderness season. Astonishingly, He used every avenue to speak to me, He also used other people to prophesy over me, and even my spiritual children would have daily words from God for me. He made sure He put His word before me. God knows all things. He also always knows what is in man (John 2:24). I have learned to give men their proper place and not to always entrust myself to them. Even well-meaning saints can totally derail you through their own opinions and scriptures quoted out of context. At other times what we go through may be a result of 'friendly fire'.

I have realised that most of the church is paralysed through the god of rationalism. Rationalism is when you choose to rely on your mind, intelligence and wisdom. People who are rational often exclude external information and instead they maintain whatever their mind has analysed. This has shipwrecked so many believers. As I mentioned earlier, the goal of the Christian faith is to be a son like Jesus, to walk in total dependency on God and do only what we 'see and hear' the Lord do. This was the way Christ walked (John 5:19-20). Jesus allowed divine initiative to guide both His heart and His mind. To fully do the will of the Father as mature sons and daughters, Spiritual intimacy is a must. This is how the New Testament Christians walked.

Intimacy is not only about sex

I discussed the issue of intimacy with the Lord. In this section, I want to relate how a lack of Spiritual intimacy ends up affecting our physical lives. I heard someone once saying that 'the heart of the matter is a matter of the heart'. I agree with this statement. Spiritual intimacy only happens when there is a heart to heart connection with God. Intimacy means 'into-me-you-see' because I let you. Intimacy is the merging of two hearts for the sake of love. It has all to do with trust, connection and love.

However, the heart can only give what it contains or what has been modelled to it. When the heart is very broken it is inevitable that we can only give what we have. In this setting, people grow up with buried pain and unmet needs. We self-medicate to find the safety and acceptance needed for deep longings to be met through intimacy with others. Since Intimacy is what we were created for, Satan uses intimacy counterfeits such as sex, drugs, food and pornography (to name just a few) to prevent us from creating proper relationships.

In my family, fear, relational distance and self-preservation were modelled. It was not safe to be yourself. As mentioned in previous chapters, I had intimacy disorders as I grew up with the concept that love equals sex. I thought that for me to express my love and affection to someone it had to be sexual. God blew my bubble and showed me that intimacy was all about the exchange of truth by opening up your heart to another, laying bare and letting that person into your heart. I discovered that openness and vulnerability are what the Father values more than anything because He wants us to walk intimately with Him. Walking with Him is all about giving Him our hearts. You give your heart to someone by being open with them. God walked in total intimacy with Adam and Eve. The Israelites rejected intimacy with God and instead got the law – the Ten Commandments (Deuteronomy 5:22-31; James 2:23). God wants intimacy with us, He is all about relationships. God will use the people around to teach us about relationships because He wants to have the perfect relationship with us.

Being Assertive in Relationships

God revealed to me another dimension about relationships. As far as relationships are concerned I was usually passive with outbursts of aggression and violence, especially when my buttons were really pushed. This is very much an Ahab tendency. Passivity is the inability to deal with present issues with the hope that you may not have to face them. I would often let things deteriorate so much without taking any action and I found it very difficult to defend or stand up for myself.

My childhood taught me how to take on false responsibilities of other people's problems. God showed me how I always rescued people from circumstances and acted like a 'savior' to others. This is another Ahabic trait that plays in conjunction with passivity. I failed to deal with people's issues right away and instead just hoped things would be better next time, not knowing that most issues need immediate action. My failure to act was actually a detriment to me. I discovered that I kept rescuing 'victims' in my ministry and other important relationships, not allowing them to take full responsibility for their actions. This limited my relationship with God as I would get into relationships and become a 'god' to the others. He showed me that being assertive with people stops this rescuer-victim dynamic occurring. These were unhealthy ties. The Lord began to lead me out of them and showed me how to be assertive with people, not allowing them to take me for granted or treat me as their liberator. I learned to say no and I learned how to create healthy boundaries with people. I was so traumatised and hurt when I realised all this, especially when my eyes were opened to see that people I truly felt were for me and with me were very manipulative as well and were clinging onto me and draining me so much. I thought it was all about loving people and serving God. However, I was perishing day by day and I could not understand why for 10 years I had been so drained. I was left in serious debt and I emptied my life to serve. My family lived without much as I gave away the 'children's bread.' As my parishioners glowed I grew weaker and weaker with tattered clothes and no one would really lay their lives down equally for the gospel. If I did not do enough they moaned so much and withheld themselves more. I felt that was what real love looked like.

I also saw the ugliness of being passive. It is actually very self-centred albeit more hidden. Having a martyr complex and trying to solve the world's problems is very prideful. I was a 'people pleaser' and had a need to be needed as well. It was a counterfeit of true intimacy and a very illegitimate way of getting my needs met. All I did could not foot the bills and this hurt my family so much. This is a perfect description of the Jezebel – Ahab dynamic that most marriages, families and churches are locked into. Jesus was not passive, passive- aggressive nor aggressive; Jesus was assertive. He is our role model and I have learned so much about this in the 'dark night of the soul'.

Learning More About Myself

Finally, God caused me to face myself in my Wilderness season and I came to know myself so much more through revelations and various experiences. I believe this is what He wanted. Some things were extremely difficult to face as I was in denial in many areas of my life. In other areas I simply did not know what was going on and so many things came as a surprise to me. It was mind blowing that the God of the whole universe was actually answering all my questions about my life. I had so many 'whys' about my life. These revelations have been so amazing; many of them I have shared in this book. He showed me the desires of my heart, my emotions and my reactions.

All that was in me surfaced as He totally pressed me. All the good, the bad and the ugly of my life was being revealed as He stripped me to the point where I could clearly see all my weaknesses and character flaws. But the amazing thing is that He guided me on how to overcome them. He gave me the most amazing tools and one true helper; the Holy Spirit. When I struggled and was about to make a mistake, God would reveal to me the strategies of the enemy and He would help me discern how the temptation would come to me leading me to victory. I had believed many lies in many areas of my life which really limited me. As I have mentioned earlier, my true identity was being unveiled and He gave me a new name 'Golden boy'. The broken dreams and the unwillingness to live that seemed to have shut out God previously, were brought back to life.

God also showed me the bondage in my life and my family. I learned that God will always show us all the strongholds in our lives and He leads us into the Wilderness to heal us. In the Wilderness He will highlight the deep things in our lives. Sometimes it can be a painful experience but the results will be incredible. God would rather seenyou go through the pain of freedom than leave you to suffer the pain of bondage.

As the sick man arose from his bed of affliction, he had learned that he had a father who loved him. His father's love was not dependant on his character, the things he did or how much he loved his father. The father's love pours out from his heart naturally because of his unconditional love for us.

Chapter 6

Navigation through the dark night of the soul

Isaiah 43:2 NIV
When you pass through the waters, I will be with you; and when you pass through the rivers, they will not sweep over you. When you walk through the fire, you will not be burned; the flames will not set you ablaze.

'I created you to bring joy and love in the life of others. You are like a magnet and you will attract many people and show them My glory. I will not erase your name'

[Seer Journal entry, 2013]

Throughout this book I have been discussing my experiences in the Wilderness; the 'dark night of the soul'. I now turn to the tools I found helpful to navigate through and overcome in the Wilderness, whilst walking with God.

Having the Right Company

In the Wilderness, it is important to have the right company in order to obtain the right counsel and advice; not like Job who had friends with advice contrary to God's. You need people who will advise you about things that are in line with God's purpose for that season. It will be a hindrance to have friends who are not aligned with God's will because they can take you out of the 'dark night of the soul' season prematurely without you receiving what it had intended. Hence you can come out still needing to receive some revelations and healing. Having the right people around you looks like being carried, as you have limped and fallen on the roadside. God will always send someone to you.

There are people who will be specifically put there to be your helpers of destiny and they will push you towards the light of God. God will always bring enough people to help you, so be careful not to isolate yourself, we all need people, we all need company and support in human form. It is easy to feel like pushing everyone away and being completely independent but it is ok to need people. They are one of your gifts in the Wilderness season. There will be those who will leave you and turn their backs on you but God will send others willing to shield you at the right time. God will always reimburse you.

Having the Right Attitude

Having the right attitude is very important. I found that no matter how intense it was, as long as I had the right attitude, God caused me to quickly move past that situation. They say your attitude determines your altitude and I have found this to be true. God encourages us in Philippians 4:6 to have the right attitude. He says 'don't worry about anything instead pray about everything'. David and Jesus are good examples; they totally gave themselves to God during the hardest stages of their lives.

It is understandable that we can feel overwhelmed, anxious and stressed but we should allow ourselves to enjoy, embrace and be empowered by this season. As I have said before, this is a time of mending, building and restructring, therefore we do not need to see it as punishment. God loves us, that is why He allows us to go through this process that is intended to lead us to elevation. The Father's heart is to see us blossom and flourish. To know that we are loved and completely accepted regardless of what we go through. Know this fact, our heavenly Father is crazy in love with us.

Obedience and Submission are Valuable Keys

Obedience and submission to His voice will also help us navigate through the Wilderness. God will teach us how to obey Him here. Our job is to always have a receptive heart. Let us be like Jesus, saying 'let your will and not mine be done' (Matthew 26:39). That is the heart posture God wants to see in us. An obedient and submissive heart pleases the Father. Obedience is key. There are two routes; God's route (A) and our route (B). God's way is the fast track whilst our way is the long way round and until we align ourselves to God's way, it can either be extremely hard or we will keep walking in circles. Obedience and submission are valuable keys to coming out of the Wilderness.

Seeking Him for Directions about Everything

The Wilderness is such a sensitive place to be in. We have to seek His guidance for everything. Wrong decisions can cost us a lot. I have come to learn that letting God order our steps is the best way because the enemy is very alert when we are in the season of the 'dark night of the soul'.

God's guidance can come in various forms, for example, it can come through prayer and fasting as well as through others sensing what God is saying to you. The Wilderness season is a season akin to walking through a maze of tunnels; if we are not receiving navigation we will struggle. Every stage that we get to needs to be directed by God detailing how to pass through and overcome. This is a time that will bring us further into intimacy with God if we allow it. It's an opportunity to be close to our Saviour and not a chance to run away for He is the only one that can truly lead and direct us through this season.

Being Positive in Mistakes

In the Wilderness we will make many mistakes because it is a path and direction that we have not travelled down before. We will also find that when we make mistakes here, the enemy takes advantage of this and can bring intense condemnation. Brothers and sisters we have to stay positive. Stay in God's mercy and believe in second chances. If we follow the enemy's voice, we will easily give up because the battle gets intense here. Mistakes are unavoidable but God's mercies are much greater. God does not expect perfection; that is one of our deceptions. We believe that we have to be all cleaned up and perfect to come to God and that is why many of us feel that God is not present in such a season because of this belief and an expectation.

Instead, be assured that God is on your side. Even in our weaknesses God will uphold us and strengthen us. God does not reject us when we make mistakes. In fact, it is in those times that He wants us to run to Him the most and cling to Him like an attached baby. Have you ever seen a child when they have been naughty? As soon as they are told off by a parent they run straight back into their parents arms. Let us be like children; running back into our Father's arms and never let go until His love is evident, not just in our minds but in our hearts.

Being Accountable

Be accountable to others, we will need to report to someone to keep us on track. The 'dark night of the soul' is a place of temptation and many forms of attack. We need someone watching out for us, questioning us over issues and decisions. Being accountable is a Kingdom principle and it is profitable and this is explained in Proverbs 11:14, (NKJV) 'Where there is no counsel, the people fall, but in the multitude of counsellors there is safety.' In a season of uncertainty and a place of instability know that we need the covering of others, we need those who will tell us the truth. It is easy to run away from such a person, but we should realise that it is love that covers, it is love that protects. Allowing ourselves to be protected by the people that God has placed in our lives to support us is part of their role for that season.

Prayer and Intercession

We all need prayer and people to inteceed for us, even more so in the 'dark night of the soul'. We will experience much warfare in the Wilderness and prayer has to be our armour. We are to ask God for those who can stand with us in intercession. In a place where there can be confusion, fear, attacks and discouragement we need those who are willing to go to God on our behalf until we win our battle. They will make the season feel easier as we are being spiritually covered, the enemy will raise his ugly head but it is those intercessors that will stamp on his head and cut off the silver cord.

The soldier depended wholeheartedly on his father to lead him out of this long, narrow and lonely road. He knew that no one was as reliable as his father. He knew that his father had his best interest at heart and that his father would be able to introduce him to great friends that could handle his new change. The soldier's and the father's hearts became connected and they were able to work together to get the job done.

Conclusion

The Dark Night of The Soul is a book that God led me to write in order to restore hope in the lives of his people whose experiences resemble the children of Israel in the Wilderness. They had been going round and round in their own Wildernesses for so long that they felt as though God had forgotten about them.

This book is really about the heart of God for his people, his many wounded soldiers who have been discarded and left languishing in the battlefields. God is pouring his heart out to us to tell us that there is a way out. That there are answers that can unlock the deadlocks and mysteries of our lives. I believe that God is using me to help those who can identify with my story and have struggled the way I have and help lead them to their promised land. My desire is to see God's people healed and set free so that they can fall in love with the God that I have fallen in love with.

I want to see them fall so in love with Jesus that their life is a sweet aroma of worship to God. The 'dark night of the soul' was written to bring glory to God's name by sharing openly and vulnerably about the many miracles God has done in my life. This book is not just about me sharing my story and restoring hope, it is a way of me reaching out to you and saying I can help you out of your season of the 'dark night of the soul', whether a mistake has been made or not. There is a way out my dear brothers and sisters.

Through my season of the 'dark night of the soul' I have come to know that this is a season in which God leads you to. It is a place where He calls you to walk into intimacy and openness with Him. The 'dark night of the soul' often looks like all our friends and family have abandoned and rejected us. I have found that many fail to realise that this is God's doing and He is actually calling us to learn to rely on Him first instead of the comfort of others.

For me the 'dark night of the soul' felt like a place where my back was up against the wall, but the truth is it is just a place where God is cornering us so that He can deal with our life. I believe the 'dark night of the soul' leads us to a place of fulfilment and our God given destiny.

I have used my lessons and experiences to help others navigate through the same places, guiding them through the different levels and stages. The Wilderness can feel like a natural and spiritual death but the beauty is that when we overcome this season it resurrects our spirits. The enemy can try and lie to us, telling us that it is all over, that even God has given up on us and we cannot move past this stage but I am here to tell you the opposite. You can overcome saints.

I want to encourage you by letting you know that no matter where we have been, no matter what stage we are at there is an answer and there is a route to victory. So, "let us arise and shine for our light has come and the glory of the Lord is upon us" (Isaiah 60:1). I just want you to know that you are an amazing son of God and all He wants is to lead you into Sonship. The stripping you are encountering is an opportunity to be purified and be set free. Things may look as though they are not working out and all hell is breaking loose but know that where the enemy has kept pushing us down, that is the place he is intimidated by the power that we carry. We are a threat to the Kingdom of

Darkness. So saints, choose to walk in the light! As in Psalm 27 know that the Lord is our light and our salvation, whom shall we fear, the Lord is the strength of our life, of whom shall we be afraid. There is hope and there is greatness ahead of us, so we must keep our eyes on the light ahead. Remember that God's love for us is far greater than the Wilderness. In the same way that Jesus overcame the Wilderness on His road to destiny, may that also be our portion in Jesus name, Amen!

Glossary

The purpose of this glossary is to explain some of the unique terms used in this book.

Ahab

Jezebel's husband Ahab is best known for his provoking spirit. Scripture says, "Ahab did more to provoke the LORD God of Israel to anger than all the kings of Israel that were before him" (1 Kings 16:33).

Can you imagine inflaming the Lord to such a degree that He would pen such a legacy for you? That makes it crystal clear how the Lord feels about the Ahab spirit. To provoke means to anger, irritate and annoy[1].

People under the Ahab spirit need Jezebel to fund what they need such as comfort and assurance. Ahab may appear to be strong but in actual fact he is weak and completely controlled and manipulat- ed by Jezebel. They need each other to empower one another but Jezebel tends to be more vicious and bold whereas Ahab usually operates as a 'victim'. Ahabs tend to be quite wounded and the Jezebel spirit uses that wounded part of them until they are com- pletely under her influence. The Ahab spirit is indecisive and can hardly function by itself and it puts responsibility on others. Ahabs do not know themselves otherwise would not tolerate Jezebel.

True freedom for Ahab is for him to know himself in Christ and to accept that identity. The same applies to Jezebel

---

1   J. Clark, 'Jezebel, Seducing Goddess of War', Florida, Spirit of Life Publishing, 2004.

DID/MPD

Stands for Dissociative Identity Disorder or better known as Multiple Personality Disorder. This disorder causes people to forget their pain and traumatic events. However, the scars from the pain still manage to resurface in everyday life as the individual is trapped at that particular junction in life where the event occurred. Adults get emotionally stuck at different ages and can act like children in certain scenarios because they have created little fragments of themselves in their hearts called 'alters'. These alters are like a personality switch that tends to give the person a false belief or protection from experiencing pain.

Inner Healing Sessions

These are a form of prayer ministry; where God speaks through the prophetic to set us free. "Our outlooks, attitudes and expectations are shaped by our experiences and reactions to life in early childhood. Many Christians have tried to leave the past behind by ignoring it rather than digging deep and laying the foundation on the rock (Luke 6:48). In order to heal past hurts, guilt and unforgiveness, we need to allow the Holy Spirit to reveal the hidden areas of our hearts and to minister cleansing"[2]. He does that through these sessions.

In our sessions we use integrated methods adopted from various streams of the church such as;

- John and Paula Sandford - Elijah House
- Robert and Betsy Kylstra - Restoring the Foundations
- Bethel Sozo

---

2   B. Goff, 'The Whole Heart Ministries' online at: http://www.wholeheart.org/inner_healing.html.

- Pulling Down Strongholds Deliverance Ministries - Ignited Church, Florida
- Peter Horrbin - Ellel Ministries

Jezebel

She is first portrayed in the Bible as a wicked monarch who attacked and killed Old Testament prophets of God (1 Kings 18:4). After her timely demise, the name "Jezebel" is not found again in Scripture until the last book of the New Testament (Revelation 2:20). But who is this second woman with the same name? Since dogs ate Queen Jezebel long before Christ was crucified. Scripture is obviously not referring to the old Queen Jezebel, but to another woman who possessed the same evil spirit. With similar characteristics – both were false prophetesses and seductresses—we can discern the same spirit was operating in both women. Today, we call that spirit "Jezebel." We can conclude from our two biblical examples, who lived in different eras, that the same sinister spirit in these women called Jezebel can live on, influence and operate through others today. It is a demonic principality that comes into an individual's life through a personal or generational background of witchcraft, sexual perversion, false religions, fatherlessness and the occult. The person involved will begin to show traits of Jezebel which are mainly pride, jealousy, lust, malice, hatred, abuse, self-protection and fear.

Bibliography

1. The Value of Mystery, Bill Johnson, Destiny Image Publishers.

2. The Teaching Legacy of Derek Prince; The Seeking Of Control, Volume XIV issue3, 1998

3. The Five Love Languages, Gary D. Chapman, Northfield Publishing, 2010.

4. J. Clark, 'Jezebel, Seducing Goddess of War', Florida, Spirit of Life Publishing, 2004.

5. B. Goff, 'The Whole Heart Ministries' online at: http://www. wholeheart.org/inner_healing.html

Prayer

Father God,

As I have now read this book, I thank you for the insights and revelations given, and I now pray that your Spirit will touch my heart and help me to face the condition of my heart, heal me and make me whole in Jesus name.

Amen.

About Me

Alex Kanyi has a special calling on his life one that others find unusual. He is called to lead a 'tribe' of people who are like him drawn from all nations to the promised land. With his openness and vulnerability he has broken the culture of secrecy where the church has been quiet and hiding. God is using him to bring restoration into the lives of the lost and broken. He is called to bring transformation and change wherever He goes with his ground breaking revelations. He is called to merge different wineskins in the body of Christ together and to bring various denominations, generations and cultures into the unity Christ desires. He is a Coach, Mentor, Speaker, Author, Trainer, Father, Business Man and a Consultant.

Transformational Coaching

As a result of this book, I was led to set up a coaching program for Christians. It's a program designed to mentor Christians in these same areas and topics the book mentions. God has trained me over time about many things that oppress us, that destruct us and won't even allow us to gain intimacy. Transformational coaching is a tool God uses to break these things, to help us walk from the wilderness and into Sonship. I believe every Christian needs a mentor to guide them in order to grow, develop and succeed. We offer one to one healing sessions, mentoring and upon completion you have access to choose and do the following:

- Business coaching
- Coaching on how to write a book
- Freemasonry sessions

Contact Pastor Alex for more information
www.gwint.org
pastoralex@gwint.org
07983602650
Address
128 Leagrave High Street
Luton. Bedfordshire.
LU4 9LQ.
ENGLAND

Made in the USA
San Bernardino, CA
04 October 2017